# IN PRAISE OF PANIC

## Sarah Cullen
*with illustrations by Mac*

London
Michael Joseph

First published in Great Britain by Michael Joseph Ltd
44 Bedford Square, London WC1
1982

ISBN 0 7181 2073 6

Printed in Great Britain by Hollen Street
Press Limited, Slough, Berkshire and
bound by Hunter & Foulis Limited, Edinburgh

# CONTENTS

# 1

## THE MYSTERY OF THE MISSING COBRA

It was a warm sunny afternoon. Bluebottles darted playfully over the weary remains of bacon sandwiches. I was deeply asleep behind a strategically arranged copy of the *Financial Times*. It was the *Financial Times* that was my undoing. It was simply too unlikely a newspaper. My peaceful afternoon was shattered.

'There's a bloke,' said the News Editor, 'has lost a cobra.'

I opened one eye. This was hardly an item of national news. 'He kept it in his car,' continued my tormentor remorselessly, 'to

7

act as a car-theft deterrent.'

'And?' I queried, full of the self-pity that afflicts every reporter seeing a wasted attempt to lasso a flying cobra coming up.

'The car's been nicked. Scotland Yard say it turned up again half an hour ago, without the cobra.'

The press officer at the Yard, as always on such occasions, was polite, and officially unhelpful. No, she couldn't say who the snake-ridden car belonged to, nor where it had been returned. She did, however, give the impression that, if any reporter found the owner of the eloped cobra, she hoped they'd wrap the reptile round his neck.

'Perhaps you should note where the car was nicked *from*,' she added heavily. Well, that's what we reporters are paid for, to deduce such subtle hints.

Ten minutes later, self and protesting camera crew were heading west towards the Edgware Road. 'You'll never find it,' said the Cameraman. And at precisely that moment there it was, a blue Land-Rover. To confirm our impression that this was the right vehicle, a *Daily Express* photographer was taking photographs from every possible angle. 'That snake's not here,' he said.

The *Express* had already done most of the leg work. They were obviously better than I was at interpreting snake tracks. They had knocked doors for two streets and discovered the residence of our snake fancier. By this time the *Evening News* had arrived. We looked quite a crowd, standing in this blameless tree-lined street. Several children stared at us for a few moments, but went away when we glared back.

There was only one thing to do. We marched in a body towards the house. Knock. Knock. Knock. The door opened and a woman's face appeared. Learn from this: if you don't want to talk to the press, don't open the door. Only the professionals can get away with 'No comment', and then only if they have a fast car waiting. The rest of humankind will be shot, skinned, stuffed and served toasted to the nation with their breakfast. You should see what a real expert can do with an amateur 'No comment'.

'No comment,' she said, and shut the door.

'Damn it, why didn't you put your foot in the door?' This from the *Daily Express* to me.

'They're new shoes, cost forty quid.'

The next five minutes were spent admiring my shoes, looking at everyone else's, and deploring the iniquitous cost of leather and the problem of shoes in general.

Then we got back to the matter in hand. Knock. You'd think she would have learned, but no. Be warned: no one escapes twice.

'Why,' said I, foot in the door, new shoes and all, 'does your husband keep a cobra?'

'He doesn't,' she said. 'He keeps three cobras.'

All this in some confusion with cameramen, photographers and four reporters all falling over each other.

'I don't know anything about it, anyway. And he's not here now.' She seemed to think she had scored a point. And slammed the door.

So we all stood around again, me on one foot clutching the other, where the new shoe leather now bore a six-inch scar.

'Why didn't you keep your foot in the door?'

'That would have been harassment,' I muttered through clenched teeth. 'The Press Council wouldn't like it.'

Some idiot then suggested that the wandering cobra might have come home. 'It's not a bloody pigeon,' said someone else.

However, as there didn't seem to be much else to do, we all assiduously poked under leaves and peered into the Land-Rover.

'Reporter in London Death Tussle with Fanged Horror,' quipped the Cameraman. The search became a lot less enthusiastic after that. What with all this zoological activity, no one noticed a rather insignificant little man trotting along the street. Suddenly, a piercing yell split the air; we all turned, hoping to see the Fanged Horror at work.

'That's him,' yelled the *Evening Standard*.

'Mr X, why do you keep cobras in your car?' — along with other such subtle, searching, truly perceptive questions, redolent of the highest traditions of British journalism.

Mr X took one look and, wiser than his missus, ran for it, me in hot pursuit. After a few steps I realised no one was following, and as a TV reporter isn't much use without a cameraman and sound recordist, I stopped. The *Daily Express* had dived into a car and were screaming down the street in a style reminiscent of Starsky and Hutch. The crew and I walked wearily back to the car; I was

9

still limping.

'Does this count as an industrial injury? I've laddered my tights too.' The Cameraman began to describe being cornered by a howling mob in a Belfast back street, all armed with bricks and out for English blood. This was meant to put my injuries in perspective. 'But it wasn't your English blood in particular they were after, was it?' I asked sweetly. Silence.

I arrived back at the office just in time for the end of the seven o'clock evening meeting, when the Producer goes through the programme with the assembled hacks. I limped exaggeratedly through the door and told the story, never for one moment expecting to have to do any more work. But I made one mistake: I said that the Cameraman had filmed me in hot pursuit of the snake charmer.

'Might make a very funny tailpiece. Ha! Ha!' said the Producer.

Off to edit the film. Between us, the Film Editor and I managed to pad out forty-five seconds showing the car, the unwise wife's interview, ending with self displaying three inches of Marks & Sparks peach satin underskirt as I ran. The Film Editor looked at the film, again.

'You look a bit arthritic; have you got a limp or something?'

Next, the Director looked in. 'Have you got a bong?'

A bong is the little bit of film shown at the start of the programme to whet your appetite. Bong as in Big Ben. (Bong, bong, bong.)

'Bong!' we said. 'There was hardly enough for the story, let alone . . .'

'One frame of film, for a still.'

So we groped around the floor trying to find one frame. We did. The Film Editor picked it very carefully out of the ashtray and wiped it. He didn't say anything. We went to the bar.

And why was this immortal epic run on the news? Because a certain newscaster had thought up a good pay-off. And the nation heard him say these carefully spontaneous lines: 'So that proves that the female reporter is deadlier than the snake. Goodnight.'

There was a follow-up. There had to be. Three people rang me to say they each had the cobra. Did I want it? I told them all to

10

take their offerings to the police. But a couple of days later, there was a phone call from someone who didn't give his name but said he ran a pet shop. He sounded genuine. Some kids had brought the cobra to him after they had heard on the news it was dangerous.

'You know what?' he said. 'I've had to feed it on milk. It's past taking anything else. It's a great-grandfather by snake standards, and its fangs have been drawn.'

I told him to take it to Scotland Yard with my compliments. But I never rang up to find out if it had arrived.

# 2

## PARISH PUMP

I was forcibly reminded of the cobra not long afterwards. I was sitting in a quiet corner of the Newsroom innocently occupied filling out my expenses, if that's not a contradiction in terms. For the purpose I had borrowed a calculator. This was a mistake, as I had become rather distracted from the tedious business of working out whom I'd bought lunch for and why, and anyway what had I done with the receipts?

Now I was happily playing calculator games and doing no

harm to anyone.

I glanced up from this improving pursuit to find the News Editor regarding me. He had a glint in his eye which was uncomfortably reminiscent of my little reptilian friend.

'What,' he asked, 'are you so busy at?'

'Checking some figures on the energy crisis,' I retorted smoothly. This was almost half true; I'd managed to work out that, if you punched 71077345 into the calculator and then turned the display upside down, it spelt SHELLOIL.

'Oh yes,' said the News Editor, pretty oilily himself, and with the air of one who has had long training in disbelief. 'I'll see if I can find you something to do.' He smiled poisonously. I smiled back and returned to wondering how I'd managed to spend a hundred pounds the week before when I only had bills for thirty-five.

Fifteen minutes later, a cutting from the *Daily Telegraph* fluttered on to my desk. 'Could you check this out?' said the News Editor. 'It might make quite a nice little story.'

Somehow it's always the women who get 'nice little stories', although I don't think 'nice' was precisely the word I would have picked myself.

The newspaper story was about Toxocara Canis. This is a worm that dogs get; and when they go about their doggy habits in parks and other public places, this worm gets left behind. There was now growing concern that children could pick up Toxocara playing in the park. It *can* cause blindness, although this is rare.

It was a difficult subject for television, because a key picture to illustrate it was, of course, a dog excreting in a public park. On stories like this you tread a shaky wire between being offensive and sounding revoltingly coy. There's also the danger of infuriating the dog lobby, or of causing quite unnecessary alarm among dog owners with small children.

The easy part was to arrange for an interview with an expert. So I tracked down someone at the Royal Veterinary College. Now came the tricky bit.

'What did you say we're going to film?' The Cameraman had a stricken look. You could see he thought that Cullen had finally flipped. I explained again.

'I don't believe dogs can cause blindness,' he said. 'It's a

13

non-story.'

'Don't look at me,' I replied. 'Go and argue it out with the News Desk. Anyway,' I continued, 'it's this worm; the kids grub around in the park where dogs have left their mess, they pick it up, and the occasional unlucky one goes blind. It's a serious subject.'

The Cameraman still looked disbelieving. I produced the *Telegraph* cutting, which had the usual magical effect of words in print. 'Oh well,' he said grudgingly, 'if it's in the *Telegraph*, I suppose there must be something in it.'

Once the story was under way, the team became quite enthusiastic and there was a sense of the hunt as we cruised round London looking for performing dogs.

'Let's go to Chelsea,' said the Sound Recordist. 'They have doggy lavs there.' It was my turn to look disbelieving. 'Are you trying it on?' He wasn't.

We drove down the Embankment, and there, in expensive and well-tended Cheyne Walk, was a little sandpit. We stood and looked at it.

'No dogs,' said the Cameraman redundantly. There was clear evidence in the sandpit that a dog had been there, indeed several dogs, but just at this moment the street was deserted.

'It's too hot, that's the problem,' said the Sound Recordist. It was baking. Any sensible dog would be lying in the shade.

'Let's try Fulham, there's a bit of green there.' We all climbed back into the Volvo and headed for Fulham.

'What we really need, of course,' said I, 'is children playing with dogs.'

We all sat in silence for a bit. 'It's too hot,' repeated the Soundman.

'I know a good pub in Fulham,' said the Cameraman reflectively. 'And it's about lunch-time.' He looked at his watch. We went to the pub and sat thinking about dogs.

'Perhaps if I bought some chocolate,' I mused, 'we could sort of lay a trail, and then a dog might follow it.'

There was a stunned silence.

We left the pub reluctantly and went to buy some chocolate. Fulham having proved dogless, we decided to try Hammersmith. We found a little patch of park that looked promising, and I laid out a long trail of Cadbury's Dairy Milk. We tucked ourselves behind a bush and settled to wait.

'Mad dogs and reporters,' muttered the Cameraman. At this point a poodle appeared, trotted up to sniff the chocolate and licked it pensively. The Cameraman filmed away energetically. Then the animal strolled off in the opposite direction and lifted its leg in a distracted sort of fashion against a tree.

'Well, at least we've got something,' said the Cameraman. At that, I saw with horror that an angelic little boy of about five had wandered up to the trail of choccies and was about to ingest the one the poodle had sampled. I rushed over to snatch it from his hand.

'Nasty,' I said. 'It was licked by a doggie.' I bribed the infant to silence with the remains of the bar of chocolate.

'Taking sweeties from children now, are we?' said the Cameraman. The child's mother was looking at us curiously. 'I think,' he continued, 'that the moment has come to beat a strategic retreat.' We beat it. Mum watched us with the air of one about to dial 999.

We finally ended up on Highgate Fields, where we had no problems. By now it was early evening, and lots of dogs were in the park. We got a few odd looks from people who were visibly puzzled as to why we were filming such an unremarkable scene. But such is the British temperament that nobody asked us what we were doing.

All this hassle was a measure of my inexperience at that time. Nowadays, I'd first go to Battersea Dogs' Home for lots of close-up pix of appealing doggies; then I'd hire a dog from a pet shop and take it walkies in the park. Sneaky, but a lot less strain on the nerves.

My spot on Toxocara didn't cause much stir. But the worries about the dangers of children catching it have continued. Every so often the story pops up again. Many experts say there's no danger provided dogs are properly looked after and properly wormed. Others want dogs banned from playparks. It's a fraught subject.

Occasionally, the story gets an airing on the News; and sure as the sun rises, those pictures taken on Highgate Fields are re-used to illustrate it.

All film or videotape used on the News is carefully kept. It's never thrown out. ITN has a large film library department with records of every single film used on the News since ITV began. After the film has been transmitted, it's kept at ITN for a few months; later it goes into a storage warehouse. Often, you need stock shots, perhaps a picture of Concorde taking off, film of a reservoir, a wheat field, that kind of thing. Or perhaps you want to check exactly what the Prime Minister said in an interview two years ago. Then you go to the film library and, given reasonable luck, they produce the goods.

There was one story doing the rounds, which even made the gossip columns of the *Guardian* and *Mirror*, that our library had film of the Strategic Arms Limitation Talks, known as SALT, under 'Food and Drink'.

Once the library find the film, it then has to be printed. The original film must not be cut. Occasionally this rule is broken, but that's risking the wrath of the gods from the Chief Librarian.

It's almost impossible to overstate how useful the film library is; many an impressive item consists solely of library material, like those regular economic reports stuffed with last year's British Leyland film.

Anyway, my doggie film is carefully archived, but what an historian will make of it in five hundred years' time I hate to think.

Dogs and children are routine hazards of reporting, but at least children don't usually bite. It's no joke at all being pursued down a street by a slavering Alsatian as big as you are. And when it's in the middle of the night, that makes it all the more unnerving.

Southampton has always struck me as a rather blameless city, with a neat town centre, a neat seaport and a neat university. But Southampton has something more: one of the most notorious red-light districts west of Suez.

I let myself in for this story, when I spotted an interesting little snippet in the ever-useful columns of the *Daily Telegraph* about councillors in Southampton considering asking for changes in the law to make brothels legal. It was the sort of story that can hardly fail, so I hastily buzzed over to the News Desk to stake a claim before anyone else spotted it.

Finding news stories is a complicated business. Reading an item in a newspaper which looks worth following up is only a very minor part of the operation. There is a Senior News Editor whose job it is to 'look ahead', tracking down stories that look likely to develop in the near future. He selects these partly from huge piles of informational bumf that is sent to ITN telling of things like the launch of a new car or the latest medical miracle. Besides that, there's the predictable: political party conferences, the Motor Show, that kind of annual event. There are stories which are developed through the specialist correspondents; parliamentary debates and so on.

The Look-ahead News Editor arranges for some of these to be covered, and then gives the file to the News Editor of the day, who follows up the stories already arranged. The latter also has to cope with the 'breaking' stories: the bomb that goes off, the sudden strike, the murder hunt, not to mention looking out for anything new and fresh.

ITN like to sign off with an amusing tailpiece, like that cobra, to send people to bed happy, and good funny stories are often the most difficult to find, and to film.

Information comes in from news agencies all over the country, who are paid a fee if they can suggest a good story. There are also the wire services, like the Press Association and Reuters. These feed a constant teletyped stream of information, including a 'daily diary' of what's happening. On top of all this, reporters are encouraged to dig up everything they can themselves, and not just wait to be given assignments.

Ambitious reporters don't wait to be offered stories — they hoover through the newspapers each day trying to find a nice juicy morsel to bag for themselves. Then it's just a matter of selling it to the News Desk and ruthlessly fighting off rival claimants. Of course, if you happen to be female, you can forget approximately ninety-nine point nine per cent of stories involving war, riot, or civil alarm.

So a story about prostitutes in Southampton was such a toothsome morsel that I was indecently keen to make it all my own.

'There's such a good story here.' I waved the paper at the News Editor. 'Southampton City Council want to open a council brothel.' This was a slight over-statement designed to grab the News Desk's attention.

'Yes, I know,' said the News Editor, bringing my enthusiasm down to ground level with a bump. He relented slightly. 'Do you want to do the story?'

17

He said he thought a woman might have more chance than a man of getting one of the prostitutes to talk. We'd need to film at night to show the lights in the windows. Apparently the girls actually did shine red lights; I'd always thought it was a bit of a myth.

I telephoned Southampton City Council to find out exactly what it was all about.

'Perhaps you'd better come here and see for yourself,' said the press officer, intelligently.

The campaign for a council brothel was being led, rather improbably, by a young married woman on the council. Her case was that the local residents were so upset by the nightly caperings in their neighbourhood that they wanted the whole thing swept up and out into some suitably hygienic establishment well away from family homes.

Whilst it's quite okay to hang a red neon light in your front window advertising 'French lessons, by Madame Fifi', it's illegal to run a brothel; so the council scheme would require a change in the law.

Mrs Councillor, a briskly attractive brunette, cited the German example to me as a precedent: the girls have their own rooms in a building with tight security. Her argument was that not only would such an arrangement remove the tarts from the streets, it would also give the girls themselves more protection. They would be less at risk from being beaten up — or worse — by customers, and they would have some protection from pimps. But her concern wasn't really with the prostitutes; she was worried about locals who were distressed at the alarming spread of prostitution around their homes.

I decided that, before I went to film in the street, we would first interview the councillors and some of the local residents.

The residents were afraid they might be harassed, so we interviewed them in the Town Hall, away from the scene of the action. Most distressed were a couple with two teenage daughters. He was grey and balding; she tweedy and embarrassed.

The girls were ashamed to give their addresses because people immediately jumped to the conclusion: 'If she lives there, she must be on the game . . .' They'd all bought their homes some fifteen years previously, before the prostitution had become so blatant. They had no sympathy for the prostitutes. 'My boyfriend hates it,' said one of the girls.

The scheme for a council brothel did seem to me to be of dubious morality. 'Suppose it makes a loss?' I asked Mrs Councillor. 'Won't it then have to be supported out of the rates — Sex on the rates?'

She shook her head. 'In that case, the money would be being spent to protect residents, not support prostitution.'

One of the other councillors remarked that possibly it could be run as a commercial enterprise. 'It might make a profit,' he said sheepishly.

A slight air of lunacy was beginning to descend on the proceedings. I thanked the families and they left. It was still only nine o'clock, a bit early to visit the red-light district, so we invited Mrs Councillor to help map out our campaign over a meal.

The film crew had entered marvellously into the spirit of things, and we planned the best way to get as much film as possible before we were chased. We fully expected some of the pimps to turn up and make trouble; in that case we'd simply run for it. A certain judicious cowardice makes for a long and untroubled life.

First of all, Mrs Councillor took us to a street slightly away from the main scene of action, where she introduced us to a couple of elderly residents who had been somewhat taken aback when the house opposite suddenly blossomed a little red lamp in the front window. After that experience, they reacted to the descent of a TV crew on them at ten o'clock at night with quiet resignation.

We staked out upstairs to watch for the light, hoping to film a customer. The light suddenly went on — just an ordinary globe lamp, with a red bulb. We watched, feeling just a little absurd; five of us tucked into a tiny upstairs bedroom, with the light out, waiting for something to happen. The elderly residents, both grey-haired, and a little puzzled by the turn of events, stood on the landing and watched us. After half an hour the Cameraman suggested, 'It's either a quiet night, or the girl over there's simply not very good at it.'

We decided to cruise across to the main centre of activity.

Derby Road is an insignificant enough street, about a quarter of a mile long, and lined with small terraced houses, most of them with bay windows. The majority are in a fairly tatty state,

19

although one or two have been done up, and the street looks generally neglected. Shops have metal grilles covering the windows. But the most startling sight was the lights.

About one house in three had a red light in the window. Beside this light sat a little toy doll, prettily dressed. Mrs Councillor said that if the doll was lying down it meant the lady of the house was occupied. If it was sitting up, she was open for business.

Most of these houses had net curtains in the windows. We took some discreet film of the lights and the dolls, and also of one red neon sign that declared 'Model'. We were using 'fast' film, which is used in poor lighting conditions. The Lighting Engineer had a hand lamp working off a battery slung in a case on his back, but we didn't want to reveal our presence until absolutely necessary. Once we had filmed as much of the lights and dolls as possible, it was time to try for an interview. I didn't think the girls would be particularly communicative, but it was worth an attempt.

The first three slammed the door in my face. The next asked me inside. I was wearing a radio microphone, a special gadget that transmits without wires. People don't know you're wearing it. It's often used for 'investigative' reporting on current affairs programmes. In this case, I was wearing it for my own protection. If I went inside a house, the Sound Recordist could hear what was going on and come to fish me out of any problems.

The girl who asked me in was very pleasant. She shared the house with a friend who was black; she said that working as a black/white team was good for business. They were both attractively dressed in shirts and slacks, and looked totally conventional. Neither wore much make-up. The house was spotlessly clean, a lot cleaner than my own, I noted.

They explained that they didn't want to be filmed, because their parents didn't know what they were doing. Both said that working on the game was a temporary thing; they hoped to save some money. 'But I just seem to spend it,' said the girl who'd answered the door. They paid fifty pounds a week to rent the tiny terraced two-bedroomed house. The furniture was dowdy, old-fashioned armchairs and gate-leg tables. Fifty pounds seemed a bit steep.

I wanted to interview one of the girls on film. 'You'll be lucky,' said the Cameraman. Mrs Councillor added, 'Most of them have families who haven't the faintest idea what they're up to. They'll be terrified of appearing on the News.'

I tried a couple more houses, and had a bit more door-slamming, all of which we filmed. Then, to my total surprise, one girl agreed to be filmed. We all piled into her house.

This girl lived alone. Her trade name was 'Michelle'. She said business was quiet that night, so she could spare the time. The front room was filthy, totally unlike the other house. There was a sofa, two hard kitchen chairs and a Formica-topped table with a half-empty bottle of scotch and some dirty glasses.

'Have a drink?' Michelle asked. The Cameraman and Sound Recordist accepted.

We settled her on the sofa for the interview. I had distinct worries about this. 'Now you know this will be shown on the News?' She nodded. 'You don't mind your face being shown?' She shook her head. I was glad the councillor was with us, as a witness to these proceedings.

I can only guess how much of Michelle's story was true. She told us she was twenty. She looked nearer forty. She was badly over-weight, and looked ill and flabby. Her hair was blond and uncombed, her complexion pasty and lifeless.

She said that she could make as much as three hundred pounds a week, and added that a lot of customers like a girl with a bit of weight. She had been in jail for theft, and before that in borstal. She liked working as a prostitute, but she said there was 'nothing else she could do'. She was trained for nothing else. She drank a bottle and a half of scotch a day.

She claimed that she worked for herself, without a pimp. Her rent was sixty pounds a week. She would not tell us from whom she rented the house. She was not drunk, but neither was she quite sober. She was cheerful and happy to talk.

We thanked her for the interview, and I offered to pay her for her time. 'Doesn't matter,' she said. 'It's a quiet night.' But I left her a tenner. I didn't believe the line about three hundred quid a week.

Outside the air seemed very cold. 'What a story,' said the Cameraman. 'Do you believe it?' We were all subdued.

Mrs Councillor said, 'I don't like this. She'll probably have a pimp somewhere. They all deny it. I hope she doesn't get beaten up.'

21

Now we had to interview the councillor herself, with one of the red lights in the background. We were just about to start when the police arrived. One of the girls had called them and said there were some suspicious characters hanging about. Us.

We exchanged pleasantries with the police; said we just had one more quick interview to do and then we'd be off.

We moved right up to one end of the street, near where we had parked our cars. As we were doing an interview, we were going to have to use the TV battery lamp to give enough light to see the councillor's face. Once we switched on the light, everyone for a hundred yards was going to know we were there.

'Why are you proposing a council brothel?' I asked, slipping into that formal interview tone.

'Well, you can see around you,' she replied. 'It's very distressing for other people who live in this area . . .'

The interview continued swimmingly for another couple of minutes. Then, behind us, a house door opened and a girl came out. She was by far the best looking we'd seen, absolutely stunning, in a silk shirt and Levis, with glossy, swinging dark hair, and a nice line in dignity. If it hadn't been for the red light in her window, I'd have thought she was an outraged local.

'Shove off,' she said.

'We're in the street,' said the Cameraman. 'We've a perfect right to be here.' She went inside again. We carried on with the interview. Thirty seconds later the door opened; and out shot an unsympathetic-looking Alsatian which bared its teeth hopefully. The Lights Engineer promptly switched off his lamp and stood not upon his going, but ran like hell for the cars.

The rest of us eyed the dog with horrid anticipation. It growled. 'I don't know about the rest of you,' I said, 'but I think it's time to wrap this story up.'

'It's probably quite harmless,' said Mrs Councillor reflectively, 'but I agree it's time to make our excuses and leave.'

The dog approached a couple of yards. I started running. The rest moved away rather more decorously. Once at a safe distance, I dared to look back. I thought the dog looked a bit disappointed.

Southampton still hasn't got its council brothel. The legal problems are proving insurmountable. I've often wondered what happened to Michelle. Perhaps she's still there.

But at least stories like that deal with human problems. There's an old, very old, joke about working with children or animals. In the news game you sometimes don't have a choice.

'I don't think', said the Sound Recordist going an entertaining shade of green, 'that I should have had any lunch.'

Nobody answered. Indeed his remark seemed just a touch superfluous. We all regarded the abbatoir, just a dozen yards away. We were following up an item about there being too many chickens around. Farmers were selling them off to the slaughterhouses for about a penny a pound. These were stringy old birds who were nearing the end of their egg-laying days. Their dismal remains would go to make chicken pies, chicken soup, or the final indignity — glue. Some would even end up pulverised into animal food and be fed back to other chickens.

So there we were standing outside the slaughterhouse getting ready to start filming. And we were all wondering why it had seemed such a good idea to try the chef's special for lunch at a local hotel.

'I enjoyed that coq au vin, you know,' said the Cameraman, in detached tones.

The slaughterhouse was a series of long white buildings; much like any modern factory, except that the yard was packed with lorries all piled to the skies with crates stuffed with cackling hens. Workmen tossed the crates off the lorries and they were carted over to one of the buildings with a wall open to the air.

Here the birds were uncrated. They were pathetic-looking things; mostly half bald with a few bedraggled feathers sticking indecently on to pink gooseflesh skin. It was enough to make Dracula turn vegetarian.

The manager of this establishment trotted out to meet us. He had the well-barbered, talcum-powdered look of a successful lawyer.

'Hello, hello, hello.' He seemed quite oblivious of our wan looks.

'You'll all have to wear protective clothes. Hygiene, you know.' He nodded brightly. 'Hygiene regulations. Very strict.'

Protective clothing in this case consisted of a white overall, wellingtons and a little hat.

23

'I'm afraid,' said the manager to me, eyeing my size four toot-sies in some alarm, 'that the smallest wellies we have are size eight.'

'Can't I just keep my own shoes on?' said I, with the despon-dent air of one who already knows what the answer's going to be. The manager looked at my nice black patent shoes with their three-and-a-half-inch heels.

'It's very wet inside.' He shook his head. 'It wouldn't do those any good at all.'

I meekly climbed into a pair of size eight wellies. The white protective coat reached to an inch above my ankles and flapped round in the gentle breeze. In contrast with the rest of my gear the hat was tiny and perched unsteadily atop my shaggy mane. I shuffled miserably after the crew, sliding around in my giant's boots.

'It must be a very glamorous life for a young girl like you, on the telly and all that,' the manager was saying. I managed to force a smile as I wiggled my toes inside the wellies.

Just ahead, the chickens were being dispatched to their final doom. Two brawny youths hauled the birds out of the packing cases and hitched their feet together. Then they were strung, upside down, on an overhead conveyor belt, and carried, wings flapping madly, to their appointment at Armageddon. They were sprayed with water; then they vanished behind a small metal screen where they received an electric shock.

They reappeared on the other side of the screen as very dead ducks indeed — well, dead chicks.

'There's one of them making a bid for freedom!' The Camera-man pointed at a bird legging it hastily towards the perimeter fence. Who said hens were stupid? We watched, mentally cheer-ing it on, as one of the workers chased it. It vanished through the fence.

The manager shook his head. 'Just beyond there, there's allot-ments. People keep hens on those allotments.'

He shook his head again. 'And when one of our chickens gets in there.' He paused. 'Well, one hen looks much like another and we don't get them back.' He nodded gravely over this instance of human depravity. 'The allotment people pinch them.'

'I suppose,' I said in a resigned sort of fashion, 'we'd better get started filming.'

This was going to be nice tea-time viewing. Just right to go with the egg and chips.

'Okay, camera running,' said the Cameraman. There was the faint hum of the motor.

The manager started again. 'How does someone . . .'

'Shush, we're filming.' I hauled him out of the range of the sound recorder.

'How,' he continued, 'does a bird like you get a job on the telly?'

I looked meditatively at the conveyor belt where scores of dead hens cruised past.

'Applied for the job,' I replied in an uncommunicative tone.

'Ah,' he said. 'You'll have got "O" levels then.' I nodded speechlessly. I always seem to be getting into this kind of conversation.

The crew had finished filming the killing procedure, so we migrated inside the factory where the birds were plucked, drawn and trussed. A bevy of naked chicks soared past on an overhead conveyor in a mute chorus line.

'Just like the "Tiller Girls",' said the Cameraman, a dreamy look on his face.

'We get a lot here from the convent,' said the manager, his thumbs tucked into his waistcoat pocket.

'What?' I was slightly startled.

'Hens. Mother Superior keeps them. She plays plain chant to them. She used to be a scientist, a chemist of some kind. Her chicks lay to order, or they're for the chop. She says music makes them lay more eggs.'

The vision of a gentle, elderly nun, scattering corn to a yard of Rhode Island Reds clustered round her flowing black habit, was brutally dispelled.

'Marvellous battery unit,' continued the manager. 'One of the best I've seen. Scientific.'

The Sound Recordist looked stricken.

We continued our tour. 'Watch the step,' said the manager, as I fell over my wellies and landed on the floor.

'Thanks,' I replied, contemplating my tights.

'You've laddered your stockings,' he told me, stylishly stating the obvious.

The next stage in this little epic was to film hens busily producing their farm fresh eggs at a battery farm. You can find battery farms quite easily. You can smell them a mile away. It's the fishmeal they feed the hens on. The air is thick with it, it gets in your hair and clothes. Besides the smell, there's the noise; a sort of frenzied chatter of hundreds upon hundreds of hens with nothing to do and nowhere to go.

The hens don't get installed into their battery boxes until they are quite big. Younger hens have a chance to move around in an indoor run in a shed, where the lights are a dim red, which we were told makes them grow more quickly. We started with the shed.

The Cameraman waved his light meter round in a worried fashion. 'We'll have to put the lights up.'

I turned to the farmer. 'It's too dark to film,' I explained. 'We'll need to put TV lights in.'

'That's all right.'

'We just need an ordinary thirteen-amp square-pin plug,' I continued. 'But I'm concerned about your chickens. Will it be okay to shine bright lights on them?'

'No problem.'

'They're *very* bright lights indeed.'

He wasn't worried, so the Lights Engineer hauled in two lamps and wired them up. The chickens had retreated a little, but otherwise seemed quite undisturbed. We switched on the lights.

It was pandemonium. The chickens went completely berserk. They fluttered in the air and ran around in lunatic circles, and then they all rushed into the corners and piled on top of each other in huge, feathery, quivering heaps. All this happened in about fifteen seconds. We switched the lights off hastily.

The farmer and two of his lads ran over to the birds and started pulling them off each other. Even with the lights out the chickens all seemed to have gone into a state of shock and, as fast as the farmer took one off the pile, another would rush back into it. Finally they all calmed down. But twenty-five were dead, apparently with heart attacks from panic. The farmer laid them out in a long line. We looked at them in horror.

'You'll have to pay for them,' he said.

'You said it would be no problem.' I was very angry. I mean, they were his blasted hens, how were we supposed to know what would happen? That was his job.

'You'll still have to pay for them. Let's say twenty-five quid.'

I shrugged and paid up. We still had to film inside the battery unit proper, where the hens were that did the laying, and he'd have kicked us out if I hadn't produced the cash.

'I've never seen anything like it,' said the Lights Engineer.

'Well, I thought this might happen,' said the Cameraman. 'I've heard of people having this trouble before.'

'Why didn't you say?' I asked.

The Cameraman shrugged. 'Well, he said it was safe. I didn't want to worry you.'

I looked at the line of deceased birds. 'I don't know how I'm going to explain this in my expenses.'

We continued to the battery unit. I pinned the farmer into a corner. 'Are you sure we can turn the lights on?'

'Yes,' he said.

'Because I'm not paying for any more casseroled chickens.' I gave what I hoped was a convincing snarl and turned my attention to the hens.

We were in a long low room, lined on each side with cages four deep, each containing several hens. In front of them was a continuous gutter full of fishmeal. The hens pecked away. Most of them were brown.

'Brown hens lay brown eggs,' said the Cameraman knowledgeably.

The smell here was worse than outside; it was stifling. Once more we rigged up the lights. I kept my fingers crossed as the Lights Man gingerly switched them on. The hens continued to peck away, quite undisturbed. I let out my breath slowly.

'I told you it would be okay,' said the farmer.

We duly filmed the hens and prepared to leave. I shook hands politely, still smarting over the twenty-five quid.

'Would you like some fresh eggs?' asked the farmer, benignly.

'How kind,' said the Sound Recordist. The farmer went to get them.

'I've got you two dozen,' he said on his return. 'That'll be one pound sixty.'

Somehow it was inevitable. We paid up. Packed up. And drove off.

'Well, where are they then?' said the Deputy Editor, as I regaled him with the story of the deceased chickens. 'You could at least have brought them back and handed a few around.'

'To be perfectly frank,' I replied, 'I think it's going to be quite some time before I can look a boiled egg in the face again, let alone a chicken.'

That evening the canteen had a choice of ham omelette, chicken curry or scotch egg salad. I settled for a nice cup of coffee instead.

At least that wasn't as bad as meeting a butcher who bought up New Forest ponies. They were wild ponies kept as cattle, so it wasn't quite as bad as if they were children's pets. However, he duly slaughtered the ponies by shooting them.

Most of the meat goes into pet food, but the butcher, who was as cheerful as he was fat, explained how some people liked to eat pony meat. 'Cost of living getting so high, dear, and a nice bit of pony meat makes a good dinner. It's very tender, and sweeter than ordinary meat.'

I knew that the French eat horse meat; indeed, in France they have a special sign for horsemeat shops — a horse's head hanging over the shop. Strange, really, I've always thought that looking at Dobbin over the door would rather put me off.

'Look,' I asked the pony butcher, 'where do people buy pony meat? I've never seen it.'

'Well,' he replied, 'I sell it to wholesalers, and they *say* it's for pet food, but you never know, do you?'

I was extremely cautious of hamburgers for a long time after that.

I was relating the ponyburger story to a gently disbelieving News Editor one morning, and putting him right off his bacon sandwich, when the post-room assistant drifted up.

Most of our mail is tucked into our pigeon holes, in a corner of the Newsroom, but the post assistant likes to have a little joke about all my 'love' letters. She floated across waving one. 'Hope it's from a nice young man,' she laughed.

In fact, it was from a long-lost mate from university. We had shared digs of quite improbable squalor, where copies of obscure Anglo-Saxon texts fought for breathing space with spilled mascara, old toothpaste tubes, three weeks' washing and the current boyfriend. Afterwards she'd vanished to South America.

Here she was in England again. I trotted gleefully off to the phone and called her. 'What have you been up to?'

'I've been in Brazil . . . You'll never guess. I got held as a white slave.'

'A what?' I dropped the cup of tea I was holding. It dripped all over my desk. I ignored it.

'Not what you think. I've got to dash now but let's meet for lunch soon and I'll tell all.'

'When's the first day you're free?' I asked, and fixed up to meet at a quiet wine bar.


'Got some nice stew today, girls,' said the waiter. I thought about ponyburgers and ordered sardine salad. Julie didn't know about ponyburgers so ordered stew.

'Well,' said she, extracting the maximum suspense, 'I thought I had my teaching job all organised. I had to go right up country to a kind of private grammar school. It turned out there was something wrong with my papers and I hadn't a proper work permit. So they just kept me there and didn't pay me.'

'But what did you *do*?' I squeaked, choking on a sardine. Julie is a sweetly pretty girl, but her idea of light conversation is to settle down to a good chat about textual variations in Shakespeare's problem plays. I couldn't see her in any of the more conventional white slave roles. My mind flicked briefly to Southampton's little red lights.

Julie adjusted the neckline of her dress. I realised that the elderly couple at the next table were falling into their stew trying to hear the story.

'I just taught. I worked as a teacher but didn't get paid.'

This was a bit of a come-down. I'd been expecting lurid tales of South American passion, all hot hands and haciendas.

'What do you mean, you just taught? Taught what?'

'English. They fed me, but didn't give me any pay, so I couldn't get away as I'd no money. In the end, by sheer luck, some reps from a British publisher helped me to skip. The man

29

who'd held me's in jail now.'

'Because of you?'

'No, he got nicked on fraud charges, but he gets out soon, so I thought I'd better come home.' She ate a bit more stew. 'I'm working in market research now.'

I leaned over to the woman at the next table.

'Excuse me,' I said, 'but did you realise your pearls are falling into your stew?' She rescued them, licked them, smiled and continued to listen, quite unabashed.

Julie smiled back and continued. 'I did get a black magic hex put on me.' I raised an eyebrow.

'Are you kidding?'

'Deadly serious. A woman took a dislike to me and had the local witch doctor curse me. I became very droopy and sick. In fact, I'm told this was a surprise because I'm Anglican, and Anglicans aren't usually very susceptible to that sort of thing.'

I didn't necessarily see why Anglicans should be exempt, but nodded anyway.

'So,' she went on, 'another local wizard came and offered to take the curse off. By that time I felt so lousy I'd try anything. He took me to a sort of hut, with religious images in it. Then he chanted a bit and killed a cockerel. He gave me something to drink, and rubbed something else in my hair. I didn't dare ask what was in it.' I reflected that fowls, hens and cocks alike, seemed to have a rough time wherever they lived.

'He said things would change for the better in three days, three months or three years. The sickness cleared up quickly, and then three weeks to the day the publishers' reps arrived.'

'Why didn't you write to your parents and ask them for help? Or to the British Consul in Rio?'

'Well, it seemed so stupid, to get stuck without papers.'

I ate a last sardine; if anyone else had told me that story I would have been convinced they were testing the length of my leg.

'Where are you living?'

'Haringay.' We both collapsed with laughter.

The couple at the next table looked surprised.

Haringay had connotations from our university days. A mutual friend had a bloke who lived there whose sexual tastes were

30

bizarre to say the least, and she used to both horrify and fascinate us with the details. Since then, Haringay has always conjured up visions of de Sade.

'It's really a very nice area,' said Julie. We were both practically speechless with giggles.

'Whatever happened to her, anyway?' I asked.

'She married him,' said Julie. 'Her parents were appalled. Apparently she'd told them all the dreadful details, too.'

My own life seemed remarkably staid after all this lurid history. I brooded on a futile dream of exotic locations as I negotiated the number fourteen bus into the office. I usually start at eight-thirty in the morning, unless the News Desk has managed to find something which means me getting up even earlier.

At eight-thirty the Newsroom is still half empty. The News Editor is busy sorting out the day's coverage, the One O'Clock News Producer is sitting in a corner trying to get his brain in gear, and a few scriptwriters are hunched over their desks staring blearily at the papers. It's still cool in the building and the thick fug of tobacco smoke hasn't begun to build up.

I breezed into the building. 'Morning,' brightly, to the security guards.

'Card check.'

'What?' We've all got identity cards, but when you've worked at a place for nine years you don't usually expect to have to prove it. The guard indicated a notice stuck on the wall: 'Security check, all cards must be shown.'

For a moment I considered claiming I'd forgotten mine and going home, then produced it.

'Thanks.'

The Newsroom was desolate. 'Anything to do?'

The News Editor shook his head. 'It's very quiet.'

I left my briefcase on a desk to mark it as mine for the day. There are more journalists than desks. For that matter there are more journalists than chairs. This can lead to a certain amount of aggro. Then off for brekkies. Out of the building again, and round to the local greasy spoon. 'Black coffee and toast with Marmite no butter to take away.' Back to the office to discover he's given me toast with marmalade. Eat it in a self-denying sort of fashion. Start on the coffee. Discover there's sugar in it. It is clearly that sort of day.

I start on the *Daily Mail*, then through the *Mirror, Sun, Express, Times* and *Telegraph*. By then my brain will have unatrophied enough to decode the *Financial Times*.

At the other end of the Newsroom the Assignments Desk is on the radio link to one of the film crews. Assignments has the same relation to the crews as the News Desk to the reporters; they tell them where to go and what to do. On this occasion the crew were reporting that, since they were stuck in a motionless traffic jam, they were going to be late on location.

'Sarah,' said the News Editor, 'do you like pandas?'

'Grilled or fried?' I seemed to have been getting rather a lot of stories in that line lately.

The News Editor opened his mouth, then thought better of it and shut it. He swallowed, and began again.

'Ching Ching, the lady panda at London Zoo, has been ill. Now she's better. It's her first public reappearance today. Now shuffle off down there and do something nice for the end of the bulletin, there's a good girl.'

Oh well, it wasn't Rio, but Regents Park's quite pretty; and it's all of five minutes from the office. That's what we ace reporters like — cover the world and get back in time for lunch.

But there are compensations. After all, there'd be oohs and aahs in half the households in Britain when Ching Ching lumbered into their living-rooms, courtesy of the News.

Ching Ching's mate, Cha Cha, lived in a cage next door; he was lying supine, like a giant two-tone teddy bear, quite unconscious that his girlfriend was about to make her comeback. The zoo staff said they'd take us round the back of the cage, so we could film through a glass panel, and not have the view obstructed by bars. There was no question of going inside the cage. Pandas may look pretty cuddly but, in fact, they're very dangerous.

Ching Ching had been ill with a stomach problem which had led to peritonitis. She'd been operated on in the zoo's own hospital, and their vet told me how she had a special microchip thermometer implanted in her leg so that they could keep a constant check on her.

32

The story was clearly a sweetie. The only problem was the people. As soon as we started to interview the vet who'd treated Ching Ching, horrible little boys came and jumped up behind him trying to get into the picture. This sort of thing happens about twice a week.

'Get lost,' said I, and other words to similar effect. No good. The BBC, a few yards away, were having the same problems.

We abandoned the interview and went behind the cages to a long narrow passage leading to a small space where there was a glass viewing panel. Here, the problem was different. Ching Ching's recovery had come right in the middle of the 'silly season'; it was a gift for papers wondering how they were going to fill their pages.

The viewing panel was all of four feet square, and fighting for space were us, the BBC, photographers from every paper in Fleet Street, plus a handful of foreign news agencies, including some-one from China. The BBC beat us to the best position, and we beat the stills photographers. We were jammed elbow to elbow.

The door of the inside hut opened to allow Ching Ching to put in her long-awaited reappearance. Nothing happened. The keeper tried to tempt her out with a bit of bamboo shoot. We all waited. Then she put her nose out, took one look at the assembled cameras and firmly turned her back. We continued to wait. Finally she abandoned all this maidenly modesty and shot into view. There was much clicking of shutters and whirring of cameras and general cursing among the press along the lines of 'Get your head down you silly, etc.'

Then Ching Ching trotted over to the other end of her enclosure, as far from the cameras as she could get, and settled down to contemplate us smugly. Her mate, Cha Cha, eyed her lovingly from next door.

The media, en masse, pelted round the cage to where Ching Ching now reclined. She promptly got up and strolled non-chalantly back to where we had all been before. My crew decided that we'd get tired of this before she did, so fixed on a good position sitting on top of her night hut, which protruded into the main enclosure. Ching Ching now chose to swing casually from the climbing bars on the roof of her cage, demonstrating that she was feeling quite fit. Obligingly she did a little acrobatic turn right in front of our camera, to the satisfaction of the crew.

The vet gave me some bamboo shoots. 'See if she'll take them.' I poked them through the wire. At first Ching Ching ignored them, but then she lurched over and took first a dainty nibble, then a branch, and went off to sit in the centre of her enclosure, chewing happily.

As that seemed to be all we'd get out of her, we went off back round to the front of the cage, and filmed the children crowing with delight as they watched the panda.

'Nice little story that,' said the Cameraman as we drove back. We were all very cheerful despite the pervasive smell of panda hanging on our clothes.

'Very nice,' I replied, eyeing the blackened knees of my slacks, where I'd knelt to give Ching Ching her bamboo shoots.

'Children and animals,' mused the Cameraman. 'I think that's the first story I've done in ten years where they've both co-operated.'

'Pandaburgers,' I muttered under my breath.

# 3

## ROYALTY FROM A DISTANCE

'Are you doing anything particular this afternoon?' asked the News Editor, with that bland expression which normally means trouble.

'Why?' I asked. This sort of query usually means another trip to the zoo.

'Don't ask why. Are you or are you not busy?'

I shrugged. 'Nothing much.' I resigned myself to interviewing a talking kangaroo, or some equally fascinating slice of contemporary existence.

'Good,' said the News Editor. 'There's a garden party for some ex-servicemen at Buckingham Palace. There won't be any royals there but we've been invited, and the Editor thinks someone really must go. Would you like to?'

'Can I buy a hat on expenses?'

'I don't see why not. You can take one of the writers with you if you're nervous.'

An hour and a half later two somewhat apprehensive representatives of the media were padding across that large main forecourt at Buck House.

'I don't quite believe this,' I muttered. We had waved the invitation to the policeman at the front gate and, slightly to our mutual surprise, had been ushered through.

We walked under an arch to find ourselves in a large quadrangle. We went round that, and up some steps, then it was quickly through a kind of enormous corridor, more like a series of giant drawing-rooms really, and out to the back.

'Golly,' I said. The back of the Palace seemed to be more impressive than the front, with a vast flight of steps leading down to the lawns. We stood at the top of the steps and stared. The sheer size of the gardens was breathtaking; it was almost impossible to believe we were just a coronet's throw from Hyde Park Corner.

On the lawn nearest the Palace was a marquee, and the grass was thronged with elderly ex-servicemen, many in wheelchairs. A service band was playing, looking extremely uncomfortable in their heavy uniforms under the blazing sun. A couple of showbiz personalities strolled round chatting to the invalids. There was a faintly reverential air, what with the wheelchairs and the crutches, rather like a secular Lourdes.

'When does the Queen arrive?' I heard one very old man ask. A young, beefy soldier with a sweating red face bent over the wheelchair to explain with rather unexpected gentleness. The band was playing a selection of middle-of-the-road pop tunes.

'Do you think we dare have a look round?' my colleague asked. We slipped past the crowd and down to the lake.

'There are supposed to be flamingoes here,' he told me,

but we couldn't see any.

'Scared by the noise, I suppose,' I mused.

'I wonder what they put on their grass?' he continued, getting reverently to his knees to have a good look. 'I can never get my back yard to look like this.'

'It's not as good as the turf at Arsenal,' I said. 'Their grounds-man told me he always uses winter fertiliser.'

'What do you know about Arsenal?' he asked, in the tone men usually take to women who dare to talk about football.

'Interviewed the manager about some delinquent players.'

'The band seems to have stopped playing,' he said. 'I think it's tea-time.'

We moved back on to the main lawn. The ex-servicemen were being helped towards the tea tent. We gave a hand and then went inside ourselves to find the press table. There were only half a dozen press there; so an overspill from the table for the squaddies who were helping out came and sat with us.

'Have one.' A squaddie offered me a plate of sugary cakes.

'I'm on a diet,' I replied. 'You have mine.'

I turned to speak to one of the old men. 'Are you enjoying it?'

'It's marvellous,' he said. 'They brought us by coach. First time I've been able to be out for six months. I've not been too well, you see.' He coughed, and ran a white hand over his face.

'And coming here,' someone else interrupted. 'Isn't it kind of the Queen to let us have our reunion in her garden. I never thought I'd be able to say I'd been to Buckingham Palace. No one will believe it.'

Both men had a chestful of campaign medals.

There was a lot of 'shushing' and the showbiz personalities appeared on a tiny stage at one end of the marquee to entertain the ex-servicemen. The other press began to slip away and we followed quietly.

'We might as well take a good last look,' said my colleague, as we stood at the top of the steps before leaving the garden. 'It's likely to be the last time either of us ever sees it.'

Back outside we could still hear the band playing faintly behind the high walls.

'That'll be the Queen entertaining all her English Lords,' said a check-jacketed American enviously as I passed a group of tourists. I hesitated, wondering whether to tell him about all those old men having a rare afternoon out, then thought better of it and went home.

Of course, reporters do quite often get as far as that central courtyard. At the honours ceremonies, when people receive MBEs and OBEs and such like, the press wait there to interview the celebrities.

Outside Buck House the line of taxis will stretch for hundreds of yards, so you have to climb out and walk most of the way along the Mall to the main gate. The policeman eyes your serviceable tweeds and boots sceptically, then just as you produce your special 'Royal Rota' press pass, he notices the spiral notebook sticking out of your pocket. 'Ah, press,' he says, in the amicable tones reserved for another poor unfortunate trying to get on with her job. Then he has another look at the rota badge and waves you through.

You crunch across the gravel, conscious of scrutiny from the almost stationary taxis lined up in the forecourt waiting to drop their occupants. In the courtyard the crew are already waiting, together with the BBC and a dozen Fleet Street photographers. The media make a drab little group, all dressed against wind and weather, in comparison with those arriving for awards.

The dignitaries descend from their taxis or chauffeured cars, the men mostly in morning dress, the women generally in neatly tailored suits, with hats and co-ordinating shoes and bags. For some obscure reason the women tend to favour blue, with white trimming and red bag. They all look round self-consciously, then walk up the steps and vanish inside.

Ten minutes later all the award winners have arrived and the courtyard is empty, apart from the press. 'Are you allowed to smoke?' asks someone. 'Why not?' says someone else. So we all stand and look curiously round the courtyard, but you can't see through any of the windows.

After what seems an age, but is less than an hour, the recipients of the honours flood out again. There is much snapping with Kodak Brownies by proud husbands and prouder wives. The crowd is promptly besieged by the media, looking for the pop star of the moment. Everyone always rushes around searching for whatever celebrity they are supposed to be interviewing, though the odds are that the celebrity will be just as eagerly, if somewhat more discreetly, looking for the press.

'Ah, Miss Celebrity, please come this way.' You cut your quarry out from the mob and hustle her over to the cameras. The steps are covered by a large portico, so it's important to move right away, into the light. Under the portico it's too dark to film.

Your crew, the BBC and sundry newspapers are waiting; they all pounce.

'Look this way . . .'

'Smile nicely now, dear.'

'No, look here, this way, now hold up the medal, higher. That's right.'

'A nice big smile now.'

Once the photographers seem to have take enough pictures to fill several newspapers, TV moves in: 'Miss Celebrity,' (or 'Dear', if you want to be chummy) 'how do you feel about your OBE?'

'What did the Queen say?'

'What did you say?'

Your celebrity constantly turns to smile at the stills photographers, holding the medal high in its case. Finally my Cameraman says, 'Right, I think that's plenty,' and we start to pack up.

All this takes about fifteen minutes, after which the celebrity of the moment staggers off, possibly wondering if it was all worth it. Meanwhile, the rest of us rush back to our offices and try to think of how to write something different from last year. And there's a sort of ghastly glare surrounding anything faintly royal, so that you find yourself instinctively trying not to split infinitives or indulge in clichés; difficult in the circumstances. Somehow you're always far more worried that something might go wrong if the story involves royalty. It's the one disaster no one would ever let you forget. . . .

The day began innocently enough. There was to be a firework display in the park outside Buckingham Palace to celebrate the twenty-fifth anniversary of the Coronation. The display would actually be going on during the news, and the newscaster would commentate 'live' from the studio on all the fun. Afterwards the Queen and the Royal Family would come out on to the balcony and wave to the crowds, and if everything went on schedule this would happen before we went off air. It looked like being a really lively occasion, and lots of people were running round the office getting very excited.

'We've had a really good idea,' said the News Editor. 'What we want you to do is to go down with the outside broadcast unit and chat to the crowds outside the Palace — ask them what they remember of the Coronation.'

'Goodie,' I said enthusiastically. 'I remember seeing it on TV, we had about a nine-inch screen.'

'Well,' he said, 'with a bit of luck you might get people in the crowd who were outside Buck House on Coronation Day itself.'

Then we got down to the technical details. Chatting to members of the public is known in the business as 'vox pops'. The term is presumably a hangover from the days when all the news readers were presumed to be gentlemen who read Latin for pleasure: *vox populi, vox Dei* — the people's voice is the voice of God.

This always makes me laugh, since the expression comes from a bloke called Alcuin, who actually said, 'Those people who keep saying that the voice of the people is the voice of God shouldn't be listened to, since the riot of the crowd is always next door to madness.' Only he said it in Latin.

Now, the art with vox pops is to be relaxed enough yourself to relax the person you're talking to, so they feel they're just chatting to you personally, not to a microphone. Once you let people start thinking about the size of the TV audience they'll freeze on you or — possibly worse — start showing off. Another essential is to be able to cut people off once they've had their say, without seeming too impolite or abrupt. All this is easy enough when you are recording the interviews and can take them back to the office and edit them nicely. But on this occasion the vox pops would be 'live'.

'You'll have to line up a dozen or so people, to give you a bit of scope,' warned the News Editor. 'You don't want to let any one person go on too long.'

To say I was a shade apprehensive about this would be putting it mildly. My imagination ran riot with the possibilities: interviewees who 'froze' and gaped at the camera, someone who ran on and on whom I couldn't shut up; or horrors, a drunk who lurched into vision and started shouting obscenities.

'Live vox pops can be a bit risky,' I murmured.

40

'Yes, well, you get down there good and early and you'll have plenty of time to pick up a good bunch. In fact, I think one of the writers had better give you a hand,' he grinned. 'Then you won't have to worry what's going on behind your back while you're on air.'

We arranged that while I was standing outside the Palace, with the outside broadcast unit, I'd be able to hear the programme sound over my earpiece. This was so that the newscaster would be able to say, not just 'Over to SC at the Palace,' but to give scope for him to ask 'And how are things going down there?' or 'How are people enjoying it?' It makes the hand-over more informal. But, obviously, I would have to hear the question.

Then I would do a spiel about how there were so many thousand people, and how it was such a fine night, or raining, or whatever, and then start chatting to the public. This would go on for about a minute and a half, but was flexible. The Floor Manager from the Outside Broadcast Unit would signal me when to wind up. Then I'd do another couple of sentences and hand back to the newscaster.

'All clear?' asked the News Editor.

'Sounds like it could be fun,' I said cautiously, and went in search of the writer who was co-operating on this epic.

'Don't look so nervous,' she said with the extremely confident air of one who knew *she* wasn't going to be actually doing the chatting up.

'I will never forget,' I murmured reminiscently, 'watching someone once before trying to do live vox pops on an OB. The first person they got didn't speak any English, and the second was deaf and dumb.'

'Well,' she replied, 'they didn't have me to help. If we line up enough people, when one goes wrong, you can just go on to the next.'

On this reassuring note we beetled off down to Buck House. The OB was parked to one side, and barriers had been erected to keep a clear space round the camera. The camera itself was on a kind of crane so that it could be raised forty feet in the air, to film fireworks, and then come down to five foot six, to film the vox pops.

41

The Floor Manager, plumply reassuring in shirtsleeves, met us cheerfully. 'Hello girls, lovely evening.'

We went and had a chat with the OB director. An outside broadcast van is like a little studio control room; it has two cameras, so there has to be a director to select between the pictures being filmed by each.

It was a really perfect evening, warm and clear. There were already about three thousand people packed outside the Palace, and the number was growing all the time. The fireworks were not due to start for another hour and a half.

'I don't think we should begin rounding up interviewees yet,' said the writer. 'They'll get bored hanging about.'

This sounded eminently sensible, so instead we started working out practical details. The barriers between the camera and the crowd had been put there by the police, so we couldn't move them. This meant I would have to interview from my side of the barrier, with the vox pops on the other.

'That's not a bad thing,' said the Floor Manager. 'I mean, you'll be trailing wires and whatnot, and in a crowd you could end up getting disconnected. Talking of wires,' he continued, 'what's this about you having to hear studio sound?'

I explained.

'Mmmm . . .' He looked me up and down. 'There's a control box you have to wear. The men usually put it in their pocket. Have you a pocket?'

I shook my head. I was wearing a light summer dress. The Floor Manager shot off to fetch a Sound Engineer. They both inspected me.

'May I ask,' said the FM, 'if you are wearing an underskirt?' I nodded; he looked at the Sound Engineer. 'We'll have to tape it to that then,' he said.

The Sound Engineer shook his head. He produced a small metal box, about the size of two cigarette packets. 'I think it would be too heavy.'

'Well, we'll have to try,' said the FM exasperatedly.

The Sound Engineer armed himself with tape, wire and other odds and ends, and with a muttered apology, lifted my dress, dived underneath it and started trying to tape the box to my slip. These proceedings distracted the attention of the crowd, who were beginning to get bored waiting for the fireworks. I could feel myself going bright red.

'Now at least two thousand people know what colour undies I wear,' I complained.

The Sound Engineer emerged. 'It's no good anyway. The tape won't hold.'

'You could,' I said, throwing caution to the winds, 'tape it to my panties. Or rather,' I added hastily, '*I'll* tape it to my panties. Anyway, do we have to do all this wiring up in full public view?'

There was nowhere really private, but we moved behind the OB van. Meanwhile, to my considerable relief, the fireworks began. I managed to pin the box, rather insecurely, between my panties and slip. 'Does it show?'

'It's more or less okay,' said the Floor Manager. 'It only bulges from the back, and you won't have your back to the camera. How does it feel?'

'Cold,' I replied tersely.

Now I was all nicely wired up, I went off to help the writer line up the interviewees. She had been wandering about looking for people willing to talk, while I'd been struggling with my underwear, so I found another handful and we got them all lined up by the barrier, ready for the end of the fireworks.

The Sound Engineer completed the last stages of wiring up. I was attached to the OB by a cable, plugged into the box under my dress, and trailing away over the ground.

'Are you ready?' asked the Floor Manager.

'I'm sure I'm going to forget what I was going to say.'

'Nonsense.' He gave me a friendly punch on the shoulder. 'Anyway, so what? Just read from your notebook if you forget. That's what everyone else does.'

There's a dreadful limbo while you wait to be cued. It goes like this:

'One minute,' from the Floor Manager.

I turn to the assembled vox pops and grin, in what I hope is a reassuring fashion. 'We'll soon be on now, it's dead easy, it'll be great.fun.'

'Thirty seconds.'

I turn back to the camera, looking straight at it, but also watching the Floor Manager's hand just beneath the lens. Behind me I can hear some giggles. Then my earpiece takes over and I hear the newscaster.

'. . . now, outside the Palace, Sarah Cullen is with some of the people who've been watching the fireworks,' or words to that effect. At the same moment the Floor Manager's hand drops in cue.

I say something about how it's all been great down here, and everyone's having a marvellous time; I begin to believe it myself. Then I turn to the interviewees. Everything goes smoothly. They say what fun it's been, how they were here twenty-five years ago; a couple of tourists say how wonderful the Royal Family is. I squint out of the corner of my eye, trying to see the Floor Manager; we seem to have been chatting for a lot longer than a minute and a half but he signals me to go on.

I move to the next person. Then find I can't go any further. I take another step, and suddenly realise my microphone cable isn't long enough. I have one moment of overpowering panic, then I move back a foot, and lean further into the crowd.

'What about the people behind there — you, madam — what do you remember about Coronation Day — did you see it on TV?'

She describes in detail how she bought her first ever TV set for the Coronation. I half listen, and wonder what to do next. I can't move further forward, and I can't start moving into the crowd because of the barriers. I've spoken to everyone within range of the microphone. I see another woman who obviously wants to speak so I nod in her direction, trying to indicate to her to come nearer. I'm horribly conscious of sweat trickling down my spine.

Just at that moment there's a cheer. I look up, and on the balcony is the Royal Family. With a mental prayer of thanks, I turn to the camera and say, 'And the Queen has just come on the balcony now.' In my ear I hear the studio commentary take over. I stand holding the mike till the Floor Manager signs that we are clear, then thank the interviewees. And finally sit rather heavily on the ground.

The Floor Manager comes and sits beside me. 'That was fine,' he said.

The writer appeared. 'I told you you'd be okay with me helping,' she remarked laconically.

'That was very nice,' said the News Editor when we arrived back at the office at eleven o'clock. 'Did you have any problems?'

'None at all,' said the writer. 'Went like clockwork.'

The News Editor looked at me. 'Like clockwork,' I echoed limply, and tick-tocked off home. Wait till the microchips take over.

But reporting royal stories does give you the occasional chance of an experience to tell your grandchildren about. And it can be quite out of the blue.

I'd spent the morning hanging around the headquarters of the Railwaymen's Union. A rail strike was threatened and there was to be a series of meetings that afternoon. I was trying to hi-jack a union leader before the meetings and wheel him into ITN for an interview on News at One. I duly grabbed the union boss and ushered him into a car, under the irritated gaze of the BBC, who'd been intending to do much the same thing, and sped back to ITN.

Once the union leader was safely installed in the studio, it seemed to be lunchtime. It was a gloriously hot day so I spent a pleasant hour drinking lager in the improbable company of a large and aimiable bishop, complete with pectoral cross and purple shirt-front, a religious adviser to an ITV company; the Producer of News at One; and a worried-looking Polish dissident. We were all deep in the mutually fascinating topic of the de-merits of the England Test team selectors when the phone rang.

'It's for you, Sarah,' said the landlord.

I gesticulated wildly, 'Not here!'

'Not here,' he told the phone, winking at me. The phone said something further. 'OK,' the landlord replied, 'I'll tell her if I see her.'

He put the phone down and called, 'It's ITN, they want you back at the office.'

'Bye-bye, Sarah,' said the News at One Producer in an official kind of tone.

As I left, the Polish dissident began a fluent critique of Yorkshire's recent batting performance. I sighed deeply and headed back to work.

Some hours later I was on a plane heading for Aberdeen en route for Balmoral. The Prince and Princess of Wales had just returned from their honeymoon cruise and had gone up to Balmoral where they had promptly been besieged by photographers.

Every clump of heather held a bloke clutching a camera; and the pine trees were populated by roosting hacks with Nikons between their teeth and high-powered binoculars in their mitts. Well, after a week of this, without so much as a glimpse of the Royal Couple, even the hardened core of royal watchers were exhausted with removing pine needles from each others' bottoms.

They therefore sent an SOS to the Palace which, stripped of the waffle, boiled down to 'HELP!'. The Palace obliged by offering a facility to take photos of the happy couple, on the condition that the media then removed themselves from the vicinity of Balmoral. I'd been dispatched by the News Desk to attend this photo session.

'We've been told "no questions",' said the News Editor gloomily. 'But you never know. Have a try if you get the chance.'

So, next day, there I was. Half-past eight on a chilly Balmoral morning; still wearing the light summer frock I'd had on in tropical London, shivering knee-deep in the heather.

The photocall was at a spot called Brig O'Dee; where a semi-ruined bridge crosses the river Dee. It's a wonderfully romantic location for photographs. About eighty press and photographers clustered together. Next a bloke from the Palace turned up.

'No questions,' he said firmly. 'Photos only.'

'That's tricky,' said the *Daily Express* in the shape of a wiry dark-haired Scot. 'What are you going to do?' He looked at me.

'See how it goes.'

I was working with a crew from the local ITV company, Grampian. 'What d'you think?' I asked their reporter.

'Well, I'm going to ask about their fishing,' He said hopefully.

'They're here!' someone shouted.

A Range-Rover pulled up behind some trees about three hundred yards away; the Prince and Princess got out and walked towards the assembled press. Cameras began clicking. He was wearing a kilt in the tartan of the Gordon Highlanders. She had on a very soft wool suit, in a brownish check; and those now familiar flat shoes. The Princess looked at the battery of cameras from under her honey-coloured fringe and gave a slightly cautious smile. There was silence except for the whirr of automatic cameras.

'Happy Christmas,' said Prince Charles in a burst of goonish humour. There was a polite laugh, but that broke the ice, and the photographers began shouting requests.

'Could you sit there, Sir?'

The Prince and Princess leant against a fishing stand by the riverside.

'Could you point, Sir? As if you were showing her something?'

More pictures. The Princess of Wales sat on the stand and swung one long leg.

'This is no good for us,' said the Grampian reporter in my ear.

'Well, I'll ask questions if you will,' said the *Express*.

The press and TV were a good thirty feet away from the Royal Couple, at the absolute limit of the range of our microphone. Palace officials and plain clothes police stood around to make sure we didn't move forward. I had a sudden inexplicable rush of journalistic nerve.

'May I ask the Princess of Wales,' I yelled inelegantly, 'did you enjoy your trip, Madam?'

She replied very softly. 'What did she say?' asked the *Express*.

'Don't know. I think she said "Very nice".'

There was another long pause; then, emboldened by my initial success, I shouted, 'Ma'am, how are you enjoying married life?'

She gave a lovely wide smile and said she could highly recommend it. What now? It was hard to think of questions.

'Did you', I shouted, 'see your wedding on television?'

'Where are you from?' asked Prince Charles, 'BBC or ITV?'

Oh well, in for a penny. 'ITN!' I yelled. ITV is the blanket term for all commercial TV; ITN is the news service only.

'Really,' said Prince Charles, then continued, 'we thought the coverage was very good. . . .'

'What about the BBC?' yelled the opposition — who so far hadn't uttered a word.

Prince Charles said he thought he'd watched more BBC. The BBC reporter winked across at me triumphantly.

Next: 'Have you cooked him breakfast yet?', asked the *Express*.

'I don't eat breakfast,' said the Princess demurely, rather neatly scoring a point.

At that moment a palace official tapped my shoulder. He was a large, very polite and totally charming gentleman. 'This isn't an interview, you know,' he said pleasantly. 'I think you've asked quite enough, don't you?'

This was what's known as a rhetorical question — the kind you have to agree with. I obligingly shut up.

Some of the press who'd been hounding the Royal Couple's steps for the entire honeymoon had bought a huge bunch of flowers, and this was presented to the Princess. She looked round at the dishevelled, dissolute mob photographing her and laughed. 'Does this go on expenses?' she inquired, showing an excellent grasp of the First Law of Journalism. Then she gave a spontaneous grin, and settled back, leaning her head against Prince Charles's shoulder.

Next they walked side by side on the stony river bank.

'Hold hands,' called a daring photographer.

The Princess of Wales, who seemed to have got the measure of the press pretty well, made a face: 'Hold hands,' she cried, mimicking the photographer's voice.

Although at the start of the photo-session she had seemed nervous and a little ill-at-ease, she was now relaxed and natural and looked as if she were enjoying herself. Prince Charles took her hand as they scrambled up the bank on to the heather. And then it was all over; they walked, still hand in hand, back to the Range-Rover, the Princess giving a little skip just before they moved out of sight behind the trees.

'Aaaah,' sighed a hard-bitten colleague, 'isn't she lovely.' He chewed his cigarette-end in a besotted fashion.

'Just think of it,' said the *Express* to me, 'you've spoken to them both. That'll be something to tell your grandchildren, won't it?'

'So it will,' I replied, 'I just hope they'll believe me!'

'Never thought I'd see you talking to royalty,' said Julie, a couple of days later.

'To be honest, it wasn't quite what I'd expected when I became a reporter,' I told her. 'I'd always thought in terms of dodging bombs and bullets and sending intrepid reports from the front line.'

'Well, how can you expect them to send a bird like you anywhere dodgy?' she said unsympathetically. 'Think of the publicity if you got bumped off.'

We were in my flat, in the bedroom, which was strewn with all my best clothes. Julie was trying them on. She clearly aimed to rival the Princess in the fashion stakes.

She'd just met what she described as a 'super man' who was as happy as she to spend a candlelit dinner discussing linguistic variations in the Norse Sagas. Given this obvious meeting of minds, I couldn't quite see why she wanted to borrow my new evening dress. He was clearly only interested in her brain.

'When do I get to meet him?' I asked, watching mournfully as she slid into a black Chinese-style number I'd been hoarding.

'Not till he's hooked, my dear,' she replied, studying her graceful outline. 'Not till he's hooked.'

# 4

## *FOREIGN CORRESPONDENCE*

I'd rather despaired of ever travelling further than Buck House or Balmoral, when the Foreign Editor collared me.

'What,' he asked, 'do you think about millionaires?'

'Individually or collectively?' I replied, trying to keep an instinctive note of caution out of my voice.

'Oh, individually.'

'Married?' said I hopefully. I was trying to remember if my best suit had been cleaned since I'd spilt half a portion of canelloni over it.

'Well, it's a millionairess, actually,' said the Foreign Editor.

My interest sank. Ever since the nuns at school had warned me about men who would offer diamond necklaces in exchange for my virtue, I've been trying to find one.

There are some stories that are doomed from the start, and as the Foreign Editor's tale unfolded, I began to develop a queasy sensation about an inch and three-quarters south of my navel. Christina Onassis had just married her Russian and then upped and left him in Moscow. Her own location was something of a mystery, and ITN had decided that what the British public wanted above all was an interview with her. I was to head for Athens and encamp outside her house.

'But', said I, 'she'll never give me an interview. She never gives anyone interviews.'

'Ah,' said the Foreign Editor. 'Go and talk to the Look-ahead Desk. So-and-so knows all the Onassis clan and has lots of contacts. All the work has been done for you. All you have to do is get on the plane.'

'Ah,' said the Look-ahead Desk. 'So-and-so knows Christina's aunt. Phone me when you arrive in Athens, and I'll have a list of contacts.'

'Why can't I have the contacts now?'

The Look-ahead Desk shuffled their collective feet and said they hadn't yet talked to any of these contacts, but I was not to worry because it would all work out.

'But what happens if I don't get an interview?' I wailed.

'Nobody will blame you, but it's worth a try. Anyway, we'll fix it all from this end. She might talk to a woman.'

As I headed for the cashier to collect some expenses, it crossed my mind that, if the job was going to be as easy as that, I wouldn't be the mug doing it.

Still, there's no better tonic than picking up a nice thick bundle of ITN's money and a neat sheaf of travellers' cheques.

And there's definitely something exciting about a touch of foreign travel, even though ITN sent me out to Heathrow to catch an over-booked flight. I finally got away the next morning, tourist class.

Nothing can be all bad in Greece. It's a country that seems to me the perfect combination of delirious scenery, nicely balanced by the gritty dust-trap of downtown Athens. The sight of the city, hot and squalid under a steaming sun, did wonders for my morale. The hotel ITN had booked me into did even more.

Every time I had been to Athens on holiday I had stayed off Omonia Square in a class D hotel that charged about a pound a night, including the use of a shower. The district is a kind of sub-Soho where cafés spill on to the pavements and a local Aphrodite hopefully twangs her suspenders on every corner. I always stayed in the same hotel, which I strongly suspected was making most of its cash flow letting rooms by the hour. The great advantage of this shack was that genuine tourists got very good treatment, as the management were none too eager to have a visit from the police investigating complaints. They made quite good coffee too.

The Grande Bretagne on Constitution Square is something else. It was mid-afternoon when I arrived, and the lounge was full of American matrons drinking tea. The brochure said it was a hotel grande-luxe, and I was more than prepared to believe it. The bedroom just struck me as luxurious, but the bathroom was lined floor to ceiling with green marble. What wasn't marble was mirror.

It seemed a good moment to tell London I had arrived. Guess what? As I had taken off for Athens, Miss Onassis had flown into London. She had spent the day hotly pursued by ninety per cent of Britain's journalists. ITN had several teams trying to find her. This boosted my morale no end. After the attempts of a battalion of pressmen in London, which after all is home ground, here was one lonely reporter in Athens supposed to succeed where they had failed. Christina was now expected to fly into Athens that evening, so could I keep a look out and advise ITN when she arrived?

'Now,' I said, 'what about these contacts?'

'Well, it's like this . . .'

They did come up with one contact to be fair, but he was off somewhere on his yacht.

However, on this job ITN were using a cameraman from UPITN, a film and news agency in which ITN has an interest. The cameraman was called Costas. He was short, wiry and given to wearing flash ties; shrewd, sharp and always late. But he knew everyone. More to the point, he knew where Christina would go when she arrived in Athens, a detail which London had forgotten might be useful. Costas had hired a taxi with a meter that ticked alarmingly.

'The taxi driver is also my Sound Engineer,' he said.

Now, under British union agreements, you must never work with a one-man crew. One on camera and one on sound is the rule, plus another for lighting if that's needed. But if Costas wanted the taxi driver to be his Sound Engineer, that was fine by me. It was already perfectly clear that, if anything was to be rescued from this shambles, it was going to be with the local man's help and co-operation. Besides, the taxi driver really might be his Sound Engineer with the taxi meter as a sideline, so to speak.

'Do you call her Miss Onassis or Mrs Kausov?' asked Costas helpfully. However, this was idle speculation. We both agreed that the chance of Christina ever giving me an interview was slightly worse than the odds of either of us winning the Greek state lottery.

'Well, she'll have to drive through her front gate, so we can always try knocking on the car window.'

'They'll put us in jail,' said Costas gloomily. 'But why not? ITN will still be paying the overtime. I've never worked with a woman reporter,' he added. 'There's an American here but she's . . .' He shrugged, with very Greek male resignation.

Costas thought that Christina would stay with one of her aunts, who lived in a suitably exclusive suburb called Glyfada. To me, it looked like the posh bit of Blackpool on a bad day. Everything seemed half built, and even the grass was dusty. But the houses all had fine high walls lined with even higher trees.

From outside, the Onassis mansion was a rather unimpressive seaside villa. There were locked iron gates through which you could clearly see the front door. But that was just about all you could see. The security had been designed by experts and managed to look as if it wasn't there at all. It wasn't till you tried to get into the house that you realised just how well guarded it was.

The house was in a quiet street lined with Mediterranean pine trees. In the next few days I made quite a collection of cones. They're still with me, sitting in a bowl in my kitchen. Under the pines the ground was sandy and studded with sad little clumps of grass that seemed to be having a hard time making a living. I knew how they felt.

There were a handful of Greek journalists and a couple of bored representatives of the local law standing by the gate. No sign of Christina.

'This is going to take hours,' said Costas and went off into a huddle with the taxi driver-cum-Sound Recordist, who dived into the cab and roared away.

'Dinner,' said Costas enigmatically.

We decided it wouldn't do to be too conspicuous, so moved well back under the shadow of the trees, sitting along a low wall like so many buzzards. The taxi driver reappeared, loaded with the local equivalent of a Chinese takeaway. The police moved in closer and watched with interest. We spread out about a dozen bits and pieces of paper and boxes on the sand. Heaven knows what the local residents thought about it. Every so often a large and expensive car would slither along the road, with curious faces peering out. We had to keep jumping up and grabbing the camera in case one of them held Christina. It was very bad for the digestion.

A policeman came and sat beside me on the wall. He smiled enticingly.

'Have a chip?' I offered him the remains. There are times when bribery can come very inexpensive.

'Damn,' said Costas, 'I've lost a meatball.'

The policeman handed back the chip paper and bowed.

'Do you think he speaks English?' I asked Costas. 'Because I wouldn't go on too much about that meatball. It's all over his nice uniform trousers.'

We gave the rest of the meatballs to the other policeman, reckoning that would level things up.

We were just tidying the debris when, with much flashing of lights and hooting of horns, a car drew up by the gate. The British press had arrived in the shape of a *Daily Mail* reporter I already knew slightly. He was with a Greek agency reporter and they were making a tremendous racket.

'Tell them to shut up,' said Costas. 'Her house will radio the car and tell her not to come here if they make all that noise.'

'She must know we're here,' said the *Daily Mail*, a skinny blond streak in a safari suit, punctuated by gold-rimmed specs and terminating in a shaggy mop.

We all went back to perch on the wall. The *Daily Mail* was an old hand at this sort of thing.

'You'll get absolutely nothing,' he warned me. 'Send a feature piece and then lie back and enjoy it. I'm treating it as a holiday.'

Lucky man; for him this trip was one of hundreds, but it was a Big Foreign Story for me.

Two hours later there was still no sign of the wandering millionairess. We phoned the airport; her plane had been down over an hour.

'She's not coming here,' said the *Daily Mail* and left, taking my last packet of cigarettes with him. I'm sure he didn't mean to. He just said, 'Can I have a fag?' and then walked off with them: devilish cunning, these newsmen.

Costas and I stuck it out for another hour, cigaretteless. I decided to give up smoking. Then a policeman, the one with the meat-covered trousers, told us she'd entered the house through someone else's back garden.

By the time I got back to the hotel, it was four in the morning. The *Daily Mail* was in sole occupation of the lounge. He waved a bottle of vodka; there was a pile of script in front of him. I drank the vodka and read the script. Considering that neither of us had seen anything of Miss Onassis, it was one of the best bits of creative writing I've seen outside of an expenses sheet.

'Stop worrying,' he said.

'I like worrying.' Well, what else was there to say? 'And I'd be worrying a lot less if you hadn't pinched my cigarettes.'

He ignored that. 'I'm going to go down to the private Onassis island, Scorpios. Do you want to come? We can drive overnight tomorrow while it's cool. The agency boys can cover for us here.'

'But will she go to Scorpios?'

'Probably not, but it's a damn sight pleasanter down there than up here.'

I liked the idea — oh, how I liked it.

Next morning I phoned London.

'What are you doing *there?*' asked the Foreign Editor. There had been a shift change, and the bloke who had just taken over was baffled by the operation. 'I don't know what you're doing there,' he continued. 'Was it your own idea?'

'Look, *I* don't know what I'm doing here.' I described the series of mythical contacts. 'Do you want me to come home?'

There's an innate caution in all successful News Editors which makes them reluctant to contradict anyone else's decision unless they are sure they won't end up being hung for it. I had to stay. Well then, could I go to Scorpios?

'The *Daily Mail*', I added with rapidly improving fluency in invention, 'is convinced that's where she's going.' I suspected the *Daily Mail* was probably citing *me* as an authority to his own boss, but perhaps he had the courage of his own lack of conviction.

'You can't go to Scorpios yet,' said London. 'You might get an interview in Athens.'

I sensed a definite reluctance to take a decision involving spending any more money.

This was all drifting away from the original straightforward interview. There now seemed to be three clear areas of attack. I was still supposed to be trying to get the interview using my own limited resources; failing that, we should try and get some film of Miss Onassis; and then there was just the possibility that Christina really might be going to Scorpios. I knew that the *Daily Mail* correspondent in Moscow had good contacts, real contacts, with Christina, and his Athens colleague could have been using a bit of double bluff on me.

Back out to the Glyfada house just to make sure Christina was still holed up there. Costas had arranged for a second film crew to cover that day, as he was supposed to be busy on agency work. This crew had staked themselves on the flat roof of a semi-derelict house which overlooked Christina's back garden. It was a staggering break in security as it was a perfect site, not just for photographers, but for any nut with a rifle. The roof was thick with *paparazzi* who had established quite a little camp up there. Most were lying spread in the sun in various stages of undress, while they took it in turns to peer over the ledge and see if anyone was in the garden. There was a small mountain of beer bottles stacked in a shady corner.

Costas suddenly appeared. He had a disconcerting habit of materialising at my elbow when I thought he was miles away.

'She must know all these photographers are here,' I said.

'Sure, but you bet she'll be out there in a swimsuit before the end of the week. Anyway, I think I've found a better spot.'

He dragged me down the road to the other side of the Onassis establishment.

'Look.' He pointed at a half-finished skyscraper. It seemed to be mostly rusty girders with odd blocks of concrete balanced uneasily in improbable places. I looked up. A small black figure was swaying right at the top. I could just see he was holding a camera.

'We can go up there.' Costas was clearly feeling very pleased with himself and went off to fix things with the site foreman. I looked up again. It seemed a very long way to the top, and I was wearing light summer sandals with three-inch-high heels. I would have to climb in my bare feet.

'Okay,' said Costas picking up the camera. 'We can go.'

I started to take off my shoes. There's no point insisting you're as good as the boys if you're not prepared to prove it.

'How are we going to get up?'

Costas stared and put down the camera. 'You don't think you're going up there, do you?'

I realised I had picked a winner so opened my eyes as wide as possible and turned on the full blue look. 'But ITN women reporters would never expect a cameraman to go anywhere they wouldn't.'

'You're not going up there. That's absolutely flat. Besides, the site foreman would never allow it. You bloody women's liberationalists.'

I fluttered my eyelashes, a trick I had only developed since becoming a reporter. 'Well, if the foreman won't allow it . . .'

'That's a good girl,' said Costas. I watched with some satisfaction as he climbed. It took nearly half an hour and it made me feel sick just looking on. I crossed the road and bought an ice cream; as an afterthought I bought one for Costas. As he walked unsteadily back to me, I presented him with the melted remains.

'You were quite right,' I said mendaciously. 'It would have been most unsuitable.'

'It's no use anyway,' he said. 'You can't get a clear view.'

I praised his nerve and balance with some point — a sixteen-mill film camera weighs around ten pounds. 'That was nothing. In Beirut I climbed like that while they were firing at me. Now,' he added, 'I'll buy you lunch. I thought for a moment there we were going to have a row about you wanting to do that climb.'

Costas was inclined to regard my attempts to get an interview with Christina as something of a wet herring. But I had written a letter on ITN headed notepaper asking formally for an interview. We handed this in at the gate. Costas started to wave his arms about like an extra from *Zorba* and kept pointing at me.

'What did you say?'

'That you are a very famous British reporter. She won't know any different.' So there I stood in my Marks & Sparks last-year-but-one sun dress and tried to look as if I knew what I was doing.

Ten minutes later, Miss Onassis' secretary appeared. She spoke in English. Miss Onassis was sorry, but she was giving no television interviews. She would talk to the Editor of one Greek newspaper because he was a friend of her father's, but that was all.

'Will she be going to Scorpios?'

'Definitely not,' said the secretary.

Well, that was that as far as the interview was concerned. There's a popular illusion that the right thing to do in circumstances like this would be to climb over the back wall and confront the reluctant interviewee with a microphone. Leaving aside any question of breach of privacy, it is not a technique to try in a foreign country with the local notability. The very least risk would be breaking my neck falling off the wall and, at worst, a promising career could terminate in a manner sudden and irrevocable. Flying my remains home would be very expensive.

Back at the Grande Bretagne, the *Daily Mail* was about to leave for Scorpios. We exchanged whatever bits of information we'd picked up during the day. He now seemed to think that Christina really might be going to the island, or at least that there might be some sort of conference of the Onassis clan there. Some of the Greek papers were running similar stories.

Meanwhile, at the Onassis homestead there had been some fun and games. Christina had come out for a ten-minute session by her swimming pool, and some of the agency boys had taken some photographs. Then one of her staff had appeared and turned a garden hosepipe on the clustering pressmen. With the late afternoon temperature still frying the leaves on the trees, this could have been interpreted as little more than a friendly gesture.

The next development for me was a telex message from London telling me that one of the agencies was carrying a hard story that Christina was, beyond doubt, going to Scorpios, but her plane hadn't taken off because of an electrical storm over Athens. I telephoned Christina's secretary. No, Miss Onassis was still in Athens. No, she wasn't going to Scorpios and anyway she'd already told me that once today. I was rather inclined to believe her but just to be on the safe side drove out to the airport.

Athens has two airports, the main commercial one, and a smaller one near Glyfada, where Christina keeps her plane. You could clearly see it through the perimeter fence wire, modestly tucked away in a corner and clearly not going anywhere. Still, London was sure that she was off to Scorpios. So would I get down there, they said.

Now, I'm as keen a reporter after the facts as any other, but when London is screaming down the telephone telling you to leave a hot and boring stake-out outside a dull suburban house to chase chimera around the Greek islands, who am I to argue?

I made a few token protests as, by this stage, I was genuinely convinced that Miss Onassis had no intention of going to Scorpios to play footsie with the media.

No, said the Foreign Desk. I had to go. I just wish they'd decided that about eight hours earlier.

Costas didn't want to go and it didn't help his temper that I really agreed with him. He said he would telephone the Foreign Desk and explain that they had the story wrong. During this argument it became clear that he just didn't want to leave Athens that night; obviously he had some scheme afoot.

'Look,' I said, 'I've told you and I've told Foreign Desk that she's not going anywhere near their island. But my position will be really badly undermined if you phone them to back me up. We'll just have to go.'

By this stage it was too late to hire a car to drive down overnight. Besides, Costas would have to drive, and he had been rushing around with me for nearly thirty-six hours with very little sleep. We decided to hire a light plane; petrol is so expensive in Greece that it would cost little more. The airport near Scorpios is a military base and closes to civilian traffic at noon. We would have an early flight down and hire a car there for the eight-hour drive back to Athens.

Then I enjoyed one of the rare delights of luxury travel. It was after nine at night and, short of a major disaster, no one would want to get hold of me. I had dinner in my room with *Dracula*, a book I had somehow never got round to reading. I cast Miss O. somewhat in the role of the Count, or one of his daughters, draining my life and enthusiasm.

The hotel's idea of room service was like something out of the twenties. Instead of the usual abbreviated list of sandwiches and hamburgers most hotels offer in your room, here you could have everything on the menu. I was too tired to tackle anything exotic, but the grilled steak arrived on a silver platter set in the middle of a trolley which unwound itself into a dining table. A waiter flurried around with white napkins. The flurry turned into a positive snowstorm when he realised I was in my dressing-gown — well, I'd expected a tray shoved through the door — and he dived out to fetch the chambermaid, presumably to chaperone.

In my sheer confusion at this, I overtipped the chambermaid, giving her about two pounds.

'Thank you, mademoiselle. I'll say a prayer for you.'

It was as well I'd made the best of the services. The Greek catering unions called an all-out strike the next day. But when I crawled in after midnight they did manage coffee and a kebab. I was told as a deadly secret that someone had nipped round the corner to get it for me. I think they felt I was a fellow sufferer, a worker, among the couture slacks creased across double-barrelled, holidaying, American backsides. Or it could have been the tip.

The hotel was managing to serve regular meals to what might be termed regular guests who could be fed at appropriate times, but, in the middle of their industrial problems, a lone female demanding breakfast at four o'clock and dinner at Horlicks time was a bit much.

Next morning we were supposed to take off at half past eight.

Costas didn't arrive at the airport till half past nine. No one at the airline private hire office seemed in much of a hurry either. We all sat round drinking coffee. I wondered how long I could keep off the cigarettes.

'Stop worrying,' said Costas.

'I wish people would stop saying that.'

'It's just a bit of engine trouble, they'll sort it out.'

I hate flying in light aircraft. It's being able to watch the pilot that is so unnerving, especially when you get one of those who keeps fiddling with his dials and looking out of the window in a perplexed sort of fashion.

'Do you think', I asked, 'that the pilot would make a detour over Scorpios so we could film from the air?'

'As long as we're quick about it,' came the answer, after a great deal of arguing in Greek. 'If we hang about too long, the Greek air force will decide to investigate.'

I was really beginning to wish we had gone by road. I had paid for the plane with an Air Travel Card. This is a one-upmanship job among credit cards as it's accepted by airlines all over the world for unlimited travel. It made a change from booking on the Glasgow shuttle.

The flight was uneventful. Costas kept telling me to look at the scenery, but I was too busy struggling with what the Americans so politely term 'motion sickness' to want to do anything except die. We got the shots of Scorpios, the plane lurching just one jump ahead of my tummy each time the pilot banked for Costas to film. The Greek air force declined to put in an appearance.

'You've gone a very funny colour,' said Costas. 'You'll need to put some make-up on if you're going to do a piece to camera.'

We bumped to a standstill on the runway. The pilot said something to Costas. They both looked at me and Costas laughed.

I looked at my livid face in my handbag mirror.

'He says wait till you try the boat trip to the island.'

By the time we arrived at the mainland village where we planned to hire a boat, it was already after twelve. We would need to start heading back shortly after three, as London had told me to get back before *News at Ten* to check on the whereabouts of Dracula's daughter.

The island of Scorpios lies off a village which is making the initial concessions to tourists. There are a couple of restaurants, a few hotels and a thriving crop of boatmen taking tourists to stare at the haunt of the rich and famous. If I could afford a private island, I would pay the extra to have it towed a good few miles further away from civilisation.

The smallest boat available could have comfortably held six TV crews. Its owner sat on deck, engrossed in a newspaper, clutching it with massive fingers as if it might try and get away while he spoke to us. He was not prepared to leap with enthusiasm at the thought of hiring us his vessel.

'What's that?' he asked, pointing at the camera with deep suspicion.

We explained. Costas repeated his lines about the 'famous British reporter'. They were beginning to sound a bit too well rehearsed.

Why did we want the boat all to ourselves? He'd be taking a party of twenty Germans round in an hour. He scratched his chest thoughtfully through a convenient tear in his shirt.

'He's got a point there,' said Costas. 'You could make about forty quid on expenses. I'm joking,' he added hastily.

'It's a pity we didn't combine with the *Daily Mail*,' I said. 'We could all have made enough to have stayed on for an extra week's holiday.'

Costas pretended to look shocked. The boatman watched all this in acute bafflement.

We finally got away after promising we wouldn't do anything to get the boat owner into trouble with the police.

'*Daily Mail*,' he suddenly said, 'I know *Daily Mail*. Famous English newspaper.' He smiled widely. 'You're from the *Daily Mail*.'

Costas explained in Greek and finally turned to me. 'It would be a damn sight easier if you were from the BBC. Everyone's heard of the BBC.'

It was a lovely cruise. The boatman had convinced himself we were from the *Mail* and for some reason he nurtured a respect for this organ. Even Costas couldn't work out why.

'If we do get picked up by the coastguards,' Costas muttered to me, 'ITN, the BBC and the *Mail* are going to have the devil's own job sorting out who we belong to.'

'If we get picked up by the coastguards,' I replied cynically, 'they'll decide between them that it's cheaper to say they've never heard of us.'

The island was plastered with an assortment of notices telling us to 'Keep Off' in several languages, but there was no sign of any real security.

The boat owner was getting into the spirit of things now, almost a bit too much for my peace of mind, and turned into a bay with a private landing stage. Formal gardens rose beside a path that vanished behind trees shielding a house. We filmed a few beach umbrellas and deck chairs that were sitting around doing nothing, then what looked like a gardener came and waved us away. He was very cheerful about it. The boatman yelled back; I caught 'BBC'.

'Costas, for heaven's sake, shut him up. I'll be flayed alive if anyone hears we've been claiming to be the Beeb.'

Further round the island was another beach, set out with more unemployed furniture. A cruise boat was sailing along the shore, people hanging over the side with their cameras. Tourists seemed to be accepted as part of the local fauna, like beetles.

We had finally explained to the boatman that I was not *Daily Mail* and not BBC. He was very disappointed.

Costas said to me, 'If there's any trouble you shout *'Anglice teleorisis'*, which just means 'English TV'. I'll try not to look Greek.'

'By the way,' he added. 'Now I think about it, where *are* the BBC?'

'They've either decided it's not their sort of story, or they know something we don't.'

'Like that they've booked her for an exclusive interview next week.'

'And you tell me not to worry.'

The next step was to do a piece to camera. This is the bit where you grin into the lens with a bit of foreign territory behind you, just to prove you're actually there.

When I got home I was told by Julie that I was clearly having the time of my life cruising around Greece and had I had a good holiday? In fact, it took at least six attempts, or it may have been more — I dried up, or the boat lurched, or the light was wrong.

In the middle of this performance another gardener turned up and told us to push off.

'*Anglice teleorisis*,' I yelled.

'Oh, yes,' he shouted back. 'BBC.' I gave up.

At this juncture the coastguards arrived in a speed boat. They didn't look especially menacing, but they were waving guns. Costas shouted across to them and explained what we were doing. As he was trying to film them at the same time, this was quite a feat.

'Just don't tell them we're the BBC,' I moaned.

We had no intention of being arrested, so meekly put away the camera and headed for open sea. The coastguards circled the boat a few times to prove how tough they were and then cruised off. Five minutes later they came back to check we really were moving away from Scorpios. There was no point being foolhardy. The story simply wasn't worth it. Besides, we were only there for the day and the boat's owner had a living to make.

Another boat stacked with tourists sailed past the coastguards. It seemed that it was the film camera the law objected to.

'You know,' said Costas, 'we'd probably have been able to film much more if we had shared the boat with those twenty German tourists.'

Now, all we had was an eight-hour drive back. I was for taking it non-stop, but Costas had had enough. We had a story. We were tired. We were going to have lunch. So we did. Costas telephoned the crew in Athens and found that they had managed to get some good shots of Christina having lunch in her back garden. That wound everything up nicely.

The restaurant was a ramshackle hut with a charcoal grill, but outside they had built a terrace, roofed with vines. The land stretched away to distant sea. We ate lamb cutlets burnt black on the outside and almost raw inside and that Greek salad of onion, tomatoes, cheese and olive oil, which bears no resemblance to its lettuce-ridden English relative. The olive oil was thick and green. Whatever doubts Costas had about my journalistic ability, he was clearly impressed with my capacity for appreciating Greek cooking.

'I thought English girls like to be skinny,' said Costas. 'All bones and no bottom.'

64

I took another mouthful.

I was glad I hadn't been to the lavatory before eating. It was dark and noxious, with unnameable pale things with far too many legs scuttling sideways on the wall. I wondered if they had much typhoid in the district.

I slept for most of the eight-hour drive, but woke driving into Athens past the longest traffic queue I had ever seen. It stretched out of the city for at least seventy miles, and in some places cars had spilled over into our side of the road.

'Public holiday,' explained Costas.

After that it was all downhill. We went back to the film agency office, where I wrote a script. I was shipping the film with what's known as a 'wild track'. You record your voice on the film sound track, but you haven't actually seen the film that's been shot, which all gets processed in London. There can be a chasm between what you think you've filmed and what's there once it's processed. I noted alongside my script which shots I thought would fit. This is fairly hypothetical. In the end, the Film Editor really decides what goes with what.

There was one curious detail about the whole performance. Christina Onassis knew perfectly well that there were cameramen perched on a good vantage point to get a shot of her in the back garden. But she still came out for lunch by the pool, although she sat facing away from the photographers.

I was fed up with the whole operation and beginning to feel like one of those Italian photographers who make celebrities' lives a misery.

At the airport I sent the film by hand carrier. The idea is to way-lay someone looking fairly respectable and persuade them to take the film through customs. Film is only shipped as freight as a last resort, because then it gets tangled up in the nice shiny new computer system at Heathrow, and may or may not emerge three days later.

I approached a safari-suited gent with a Gucci briefcase. 'I'm from ITN. We've got some newsfilm to go to London. Would you mind taking it?' Sure — what did he have to do?

'When you land, go through the red channel — the "something to declare" area, and a bloke from Shands, that's a film shipping agency, will meet you and take the film. He'll have all the clearance papers. I'll speak to customs this end.'

Although the new screening equipment allegedly isn't supposed to damage film or magnetic tape, reporters are very superstitious about it and don't like to put film through it. Because the film cans are sealed — and can't be opened except in a darkroom — customs at embarkation need to be reassured you're up to nothing illegal.

The first man I approached had suddenly got very uneasy when I mentioned the red channel. Up to that point he'd been quite happy to take the film. 'No, no, just remembered I've got to dash at the other end . . .' He backed off in evident alarm.

I've since occasionally wondered what it was he was smuggling. I could hardly tell him that carrying newsfilm gives a convincing air of innocence.

In the end a nice man in advertising accepted it.

As I was going to be at the airport, London asked me to check out the condition of British passengers stranded by an air traffic dispute. There were only a couple of hundred, and the longest any of them had been there was twelve hours. This wasn't enough to warrant a story. I'd been stranded myself for thirty-six hours a few weeks previously on holiday to Crete, so hard luck tales were falling on fairly deaf ears.

However, I bought scores of cups of coffee, and said I'd be back that night. If they were still there we'd do a film. I did give one couple a tenner. They had a couple of kids and were flat broke. The airline officials just looked blank when asked about food for the children.

They all eventually took off a few hours later. It was sad, but hardly news.

What *was* news was an earthquake in Salonika. Whole towns had been half flattened and the population had fled from the remaining buildings. According to the Greek media, people were terrified to go to their homes in case they collapsed around them so were living in miles of tents. Very few people had actually been killed, but much of the north of Greece was a vast refugee camp. Constant slight tremors kept the panic well inflamed. The Greek press was totally taken up with the story, and people in the street, seeing I was British with a film team, kept asking, 'Why don't you go to Salonika?'

'Can I go?' I asked London. It would have meant hiring yet

another plane and would have taken two days. Most of the best material would be shot in the evening, as the flames from make-shift cooking fires were said to light the sky for miles. 'It'll be very human interest,' I said.

'No,' said London. If I was up in Salonika filming earthquake victims, I couldn't be watching Christina, could I? Besides, hardly anyone had died. At the hotel the desk clerk wanted to know if I was going north. Nobody seemed to understand why we weren't interested in the quake. I didn't understand myself, so what could I tell them? The outside world just didn't want to know.

Back at the Onassis shack, I did a little film about the inquisitive photographers hanging about. We knew quite a few of them by now so they obligingly posed in assorted precarious locations. Then I phoned the office and said that I was never going to get an interview so could I please, please, come home.

'Next flight you can get on,' they replied.

I bought Costas a last drink and said goodbye, then spent the next morning just sitting in a café in Constitution Square watching the tourists and waiting until it was time for the plane. Foreign Desk had sent a telegram of congratulations for the Onassis story. It had run on two Sunday bulletins, for slightly less than two minutes.. 'Thanks hard work,' the telegram had read.

There was one bonus: all the tourist-class seats to London were booked up for weeks, so I had to fly home first class.

As the Olympic Airways jet took off for Heathrow, Christina left her house to return to Moscow. Perhaps she'd just been waiting for me to go?

In Salonika the refugees prepared for another night in the tents. It would be some time before *they'd* be going home.

But the amount of travelling I was doing for the company wasn't really going far to satisfy a positively maniacal love of trains and planes. My taste for expensive holidays was a bit curtailed at this juncture, because I had finally decided to buy a flat and was busily stacking away the shekels in an attempt to get a deposit together. Unfortunately, as fast as I tried to save, the price of flats always kept just one jump ahead. I began to feel like a donkey chasing after a carrot held over its nose on a pole.

Meanwhile, my Islington flat ate up cash at the rate of thirty quid a week, to say nothing of heating costs. I had saved up a few pounds in my 'China Fund' — my immediate ambition being a trip there — but this now moved over into the 'buying a home of my own' section of my personal economy.

All in all, I was pretty fed up. There seemed no immediate possibility of another nice exotic trip from ITN and no prospect of financing myself anywhere further than Brighton for about another year. By then I hoped I'd have a roof of my own over my head and a slightly more stable bank balance.

Just to make that particular day quite perfect, it was pouring with rain, there was nothing on TV and I hadn't any books I hadn't read at least three times. I was broke, bored and couldn't finish the *Telegraph* crossword. There were quite a number of things I could have been doing — like giving the bath a much needed scouring, or washing the kitchen floor — but these diversions somehow seemed to lack their usual glamorous appeal. I settled down to watch *Tom and Jerry* — a final admission of surrender to total inactivity.

When the telephone went I nearly didn't answer it. I had reached that stage of relaxation where, if the Second Coming happened in my back garden, I'd wait to see it decently reported by someone else on the TV news. But the phone rang on and on. I levered myself off the sofa and made a languid grab at the receiver.

It was my cousin David, who has a business travel firm, arranging conferences in foreign parts.

'I'm bringing out a brochure about the firm,' he said, after the usual preliminaries of 'How's your Mum?' and 'How's your Dad?'. 'I thought it would be nice to have a travel article in it, describing a visit to a trade fair. Perhaps the Düsseldorf Plastics Fair. Would you like to do it?'

Well, the Düsseldorf Plastics Fair may not be your idea of heaven, but at least it would be an extremely welcome change of scene.

'We were going to get Paul Callan to do it,' he continued with cousinly honesty, 'but then it occurred to me we'd have to *pay* Paul Callan.'

'Thanks.'

68

'Don't mention it,' said David.

Working freelance, even for your cousin, means getting an okay from ITN. This wasn't difficult, and the next thing on the menu was the arrival of David at the flat, complete with about a hundred brochures on his company's services plus a wodge of expenses.

'We're putting you up in the Nikko,' he said. 'Japanese hotel, really marvellous.' This sounded good, but I did have one slight lingering doubt.

'David, you know this won't be exactly advertising copy I write. You might not like it.'

He waved this aside. I still had doubts, but after this token protest felt able to wave him goodbye with a clear, well clearish, conscience.

The only other woman on the flight was a long thin embodiment of continental chic. I watched gloomily as all the flash young executives fell over themselves to carry her burgundy pigskin slimline briefcase complete with combination locks.

I smoothed down my antique tweed suit and wished I was wearing half a stone less round my plimsoll line. My own battered document case, the survivor of numerous catastrophes, tucked itself away modestly under my seat and glared across at glamour girl's pigskin delight.

Glamour girl got six foot of Nordic blond in the seat next to her; I got a fat man from Bradford who spent the flight drinking double scotches — this at nine-thirty in the morning. It's not that I object to fat. It was his dandruff I didn't like.

'And where are you going to, love?'

He stretched out as if he were going to pat my knee, but his hand sort of thought better of it and hovered in space. A little shower of dandruff drifted down.

'The plastics fair at Düsseldorf,' I replied rather self-consciously. At that the fat man became even more cheerful, that was where he was going and he'd see me there, wouldn't he? And incidentally, hadn't he seen me somewhere before? I smiled sweetly. He settled back and pretended to read the *Economist*.

At Düsseldorf I slid out of the airport waving to Fatty whom I overtook and passed at speed, on the way through passport control. Then off to the hotel. But a snag — cousin David hadn't booked me into the Nikko after all, but into a distinctly less grand establishment whose main claim to notoriety was that it overlooked the all-night tram track. Trams can be very noisy at three in the morning, especially when your room — with single glazing — faces straight on to them.

The Düsseldorf trade fair complex is worth a visit just for itself. It covers a vast area — dozen of huge halls are connected by see-through overhead tunnels with moving walkways. Under this web of glass and plastic is an amazing patio — the size of several football pitches. This is dotted with tents and stands, anchored barrage balloons and so forth.

The organisers issued the press with pedometers to give some idea of the mileage (kilometrage) covered by the average fair visitor.

'Don't know why they bothered,' moaned a worn-looking British delegate. 'They could measure it in poundage, I've dropped nearly a stone.'

The first thing a reporter does when he arrives at a trade fair, be it the Düsseldorf Plastics Fair or the Motor Show in Birmingham, is to head for the press room. Here are stacked piles of information from all the manufacturers who are showing their products. Here, too, are helpful press agents who'll explain everything in words of one syllable and, with luck, help you to avoid doing too much hard work.

Most press rooms at least provide you with a free cup of coffee, and the very classy ones occasionally with something stronger. Many a lucid report on the future of some branch of British industry has been written by experienced souls who put their feet up and talk to people in the bar, rather than waste valuable energy trotting round a score of display stands. Sometimes you even get free goodies. The Motor Show is especially hot on this, with smart little models of 'James Bond' cars dished out.

At Düsseldorf a machine on one stand turned out plastic pigs, hundreds of them, with slots at around the best back bacon level in which to put your spare pfennigs. Scores of (presumably) top executives clustered hungrily around this clone factory, though whether to admire the machine's performance or pick up a little free something for the infants back home was open to question.

70

Just about every other delegate that day seemed to be clutching a pig.

The restaurant in the conference centre was like restaurants in conference centres the world over — the spacemobile exterior hadn't extended to the cuisine. I ate a very small, very expensive, chicken salad, only relieved by the fact that, although it was half-past three, Germany doesn't have licensing hours and even conference centre canteens can produce something pleasantly alcoholic to disguise the food.

In the front hall of the centre, Arab businessmen shuttled in and out of a Moslem prayer room. I wasn't sure if it was okay for women to go in, but slid up to the door to glimpse a prayer mat and framed scripts on the walls, presumably verses from the Koran. Out of perverse curiosity, I tried the door of the Christian chapel a bit further down. Predictably, that was locked.

The non-teetotal creeds seemed to be doing much of their business in the bar. You began to recognise a trade-fair face in the streets of the city. They all wore the same white, strained, exhausted look compounded of gin and panic.

But some companies at Düsseldorf clearly kept expenses tight. Dotted round the huge exhibition halls were little barrows selling bread and delicious-looking hot sausage. These were besieged by pools of mohair-suited city types, talking in millions of dollars as they chumped their hot dogs. Or perhaps this was just a light between-meals snack. There were barrows selling iced beer too, in half-litre bottles. You don't get that at the Birmingham Motor Show.

After I'd worn my high heels down about half an inch exploring the conference centre, I turned my attention to Düsseldorf itself. It's an incredibly smart city with a canal running through the main street. The *strasse* is lined with the most pricey shops, like Bond Street writ larger and more colourful. I thought it the most elegant shopping street I'd ever seen. I had completely run out of reading material so did a little light shopping at a local bookshop; no problem finding one that sold the latest English books.

Then I sat in a brasserie which was more like an Englishwoman's fantasy of a Paris café than anything you'd be likely to find on the Left Bank. No Americans for one thing; it's not on the tourist circuit. The café was wood-lined in dark expensive colours with tables on different levels; a kind of illuminated tickertape flashed the latest news above the bar. I drank coffee and wished I'd worn my best suit.

I didn't quite have the nerve to venture out for dinner, so ate in the hotel. Snails. I love snails when someone else is paying my expenses. A German delegate, almost exaggeratedly tall and blond, began the evening's entertainment by attempting a little mild seduction.

'Ah, well,' he said, repulsed. 'In two years' time the next conference is in Birmingham. Perhaps in Birmingham?'

'Birmingham, where else?' I muttered.

As the evening wore on, I began to think I should have hung on to this relatively house-trained Lothario for a chaperone. I didn't particularly want to go to bed early, so settled down in the hotel lounge with my book. I had changed for dinner and was wearing a dress which covered me from neck to wrist to ankle and would have passed an ayatollah's strictures. So the ensuing events were inexplicable.

Another bloke sidled into the lounge and parked himself in the chair next to me. I looked up and nodded, then returned to my book.

'Will you come and have dinner?' he opened proceedings.

I looked at him again; he wore a snappy jacket which contrasted nicely with features set in the sort of expression considered excessively gloomy at a family funeral. 'Thank you, I've eaten already.'

'Well, will you come with me while I eat?'

I raised an eyebrow. I'm very good at raising eyebrows. I used to practise in front of a mirror. I'm sorry I can't waggle my ears in spite of considerable effort.

The raised eyebrow didn't work, so I was more explicit. 'Thank you, but I am reading.' I started to look round for one of the hotel staff, but the place was deserted.

'You are English?' I nodded. 'And have you come from London just for the conference?' I nodded again. I thought I was beginning to get the drift.

'You are very pretty. It would be five hundred pounds in your money. Or I have marks and dollars.' I could feel my eyebrows elevate into elaborate question-marks.

'I've told you, I am reading. Now please leave or I will call the manager.'

He looked at me again. Either his understanding of English was rather less good than his speech, or he was more drunk than he appeared. His eyes had all the dynamic enthusiasm of damp marbles.

'A thousand pounds. And that's my last offer.'

I didn't know whether to be outraged or flattered.

'Look, you are making a mistake, now would you kindly leave me alone,' I said with exaggerated politeness.

He looked puzzled and did now seem to be a bit drunk. I was beginning to get alarmed that the situation was going to get nasty. There was still no one else in the lounge. I got up to go; he tugged my sleeve.

'A thousand pounds is far more than the rate,' he said. 'Why did you come from London? You won't get better there.'

I finally decided to be explicit. 'I hate to break the news, but I am a journalist. Journalist. Reporter. I am here to write a report about the plastics fair.' He stared at me blankly, not even a faint glint of intelligence on his sweaty face.

'One thousand five hundred pounds.' I pulled my sleeve from his grip and sprinted out of the lounge, then steadied to walk decorously to the reception desk.

'There is a bloke in your lounge making indecent propositions. Will you have him thrown out?' The receptionist stared, then the manager appeared, so I had to explain again what had happened.

I was in mid-tale, when who should materialise by my side but my little friend.

'Fifteen hundred pounds,' he said hopefully.

The manager stepped hastily between us and an angry conversation followed. I retreated to the lounge.

The manager came in and apologised. 'He was drunk. And you know, it is unusual for a woman to be alone at these trade fairs. You realise what he thought?' I nodded. I sat in the lounge for ten minutes more to make my point, then went to bed and lay awake listening to the trams.

It wouldn't happen in Birmingham, I hope.

This little variation on an age-old theme had rather distracted me from the matter in hand. When I described it to my cousin's rep at the conference centre the next day, she told with guilty glee how she had once misunderstood the meaning of some delegates who had asked her for a place for a 'good night out' and had dispatched them to a local *maison* of ill repute. The good night out they had in mind had been more along the lines of a decent meal with perhaps an innocent bit of nightclubbing thrown in. What might loosely be described as a diplomatic incident followed, complicated because, officially, in Düsseldorf there is no such thing as a brothel.

I decided that what this story now needed was some healthy activity, a kind of mental equivalent of a bracing cold shower. '

As luck would have it, just thirty miles from Düsseldorf, in Cologne, a sports fair was in progress. I travelled there by train, sharing the compartment with yet another plastics fair delegate, this one fortunately docile.

Once in Cologne, there was the fun of trying to find the hotel where I'd arranged to meet my guide. The ancient cathedral broods over the *bahnhof*, and both are surrounded by a pedestrian precinct. This was all well and good, but the hotel I was trying to reach was beyond the precinct. A taxi said it was too short a trip, but there seemed to be no way at all to get past the high concrete barriers surrounding the walkway, and attain the hotel.

Finally, after a full forty minutes of aimless wandering, I tucked my dignity out of sight, hitched up my skirt and climbed over the four-foot barrier. I'm sure that sort of thing never happens to lady barristers.

The sports fair was in yet another conference centre, not nearly as impressive as the Düsseldorf space-station, just a collection of barn-like halls.

The first stand was surrounded by executives trying sweatily to put a basket ball through a net. Well, all that netball at my horrible school had to be good for something. Elbowing the unfit executives aside, I nonchalantly scored a hat-trick. This, I privately admitted to myself, was mostly a matter of luck. I took a bow — then found I had won three netballs. I now know just how the Ancient Mariner felt about his albatross; I couldn't get rid of the things.

When I went for coffee, I tucked them well under the table and forgot them, only to be pursued by a beaming waiter waving armfuls of netball. What's more I had to tip him.

So, thus encumbered, it was down to the ground floor where they were selling saunas and fancy baths, filled with foaming bubbles, sometimes artistically coloured. By late afternoon, the suds looked chilly and unappetising. A model in a leotard, moulded to outline her navel and a good deal else besides, exercised lethargically on some gymnastic equipment. Every man who went past tried unsuccessfully to look as if he were just interested in the hardware.

'Very stable frame that,' murmured a voice at my ear. Its owner's eyes were riveted on the lurching cleavage.

I removed my inadequate form from such competition. It's difficult to look elegant clutching three netballs. By way of compensation, I bought a pocket chess set in the games section, and then dropped the pieces all over the floor. All the chessmen were tiny — half the size of a fingernail — so about a score of delegates helped me spend an entertaining ten minutes crawling under stands, trying to pick up the bits. I took advantage of the confusion to stuff the netballs securely out of sight under a table.

The flight back was packed with execs clutching plastic bags full of trade literature and free gifts. An occasional plastic pig strolled past and a netball broke free from cover and bounced round the check-in hall. Miss Pigskin Briefcase was on the same flight; after the revelations in the hotel, I indulged in some viciously uncharitable thoughts.

At the duty-free counter it was easy to spot the blokes on the make: they buy two bottles of scent — both in the same flavour. There's nothing gives hubby away more quickly than a breath of Je Reviens, when the Missus wears Miss Dior.

The traditional taxi shortage at Heathrow meant sharing with a businessman from the Soviet Union. He was just back from yet a third trade fair, Phototechnik. Even the Russians are in on it. We dropped him off just at the street entrance of the Soviet enclave in North London — for some reason he didn't want to be taken right to the front door. Then home.

The front door of the flat seemed stuck, so I had to put all my weight on it to force it open. Something felt wrong. I walked in. The kitchen door had been smashed open and my cupboards were ajar, with bags and clothes tipped over the floor.

Burgled.

I gave way to a wholly rational feeling of panic, standing frozen for a good thirty seconds before trying to phone the police. Line out of order. It would be. Then I raced upstairs and proceeded to have a nice comforting attack of hysterics on the woman in the flat above.

The police arrived in a few moments and strolled around the flat making cheerful comments like 'Must have been kids', 'Easy flat to get into, this', and so on.

I called a locksmith. He was quite happy to climb out of bed and mend my front door in the middle of the night, but it would be sixty quid. Well, I wasn't going to sleep with no door lock. By the time I finally got to bed, a new flat had moved from being top on my list of priorities to being just about my only priority.

Next day I settled down to writing an account of my adventures in Düsseldorf. I thought the incident in the hotel lounge had better be excluded. It might give people the wrong idea about the services they could expect my cousin to provide. I duly typed up my article and phoned David. Besides my story, I had also brought back some photographs which he needed for the new brochure, so I packed everything up and gave them to the motor-cycle dispatch rider my cousin sent round.

Somewhere between my flat and his office the envelope somehow managed to detach itself from the back of the bike and pass into the fourth dimension. Vanished. Totally and without trace. To make matters worse, I had committed the cardinal sin for any journalist — I hadn't taken a copy of my article. So I had to write it all over again. Still, it broke the monotony.

The difference between doing this written review of a trade fair and making a TV news film of a similar event was very revealing. All I had had to do in Germany was shuffle around the various displays clutching a pencil and taking notes. And there were no deadlines.

From a filming point of view, exhibitions can turn into a cata-logue of disasters. It's difficult to give an idea of the sheer size of an exhibition hall, and the places are always packed solid, so people are continually falling over the lighting cables. And, instead of a notebook, you are using all the paraphernalia of a TV team.

Even the most brilliantly lit hall needs back-up lighting for a film camera. It's doing the lighting that takes time on these expeditions. The Lights Engineer has to meet the house electrician in whatever premises you're filming. TV lights can be plugged into ordinary thirteen-amp sockets, just like the ones at home. But you'd be surprised how many places don't have thirteen-amp sockets, but have weird and wonderful contraptions of their own. Like at a London water treatment centre, where the equipment baffled even our electrician. 'Never seen anything like it,' he muttered as he rewired right back to the fuse box.

Once the Lights Man has found a point, it's not just a matter of plugging in and switching on. The point can be yards away from where you want to film, so the whole area ends up festooned with extension cables.

As the lights themselves aren't wonderfully stable, it only needs an inquisitive little boy, or his dad, to give the cable a tug, and you're surrounded by broken glass. And those cables do seem to snake off looking for trouble. Once the lights are finally set up, they have to be moved for each new shot.

At the Motor Show — a relatively easy job in the new Birmingham conference centre, which has a lot of power points — you need one lighting set-up to film, say, Ford, then you have to move the whole thing over about a hundred yards to start on British Leyland.

All this gear is shifted by one man, so it's not exactly an instant performance. For a 'quick burst', light can be supplied by a hand lamp run off batteries. This is usually used outside — to give daylight a bit of help, but, in a rush, can be used indoors. But hand lamps aren't much good when filming anything on the scale of a motor show.

Trade shows are further complicated by the timing arrangements. The Motor Show, for instance, has a press day before the main opening, so the TV news can show film of it the day before the show is open to the public.

I arrived at the Birmingham centre at half past eight in the morning, to find most of the stands still only half finished. I was supposed to get a report back for *News at One*.

I was sending the story from the Birmingham TV station; it would be processed and edited at ATV, then would go to London on a system a bit like a phone line but with pictures. London would record and then replay it on *News at One*. The opportunities for slips en route are legion.

Anyway, at nine o'clock the stands still aren't finished. Now, no News Editor worth his salt will take this as an explanation for a non-existent story — that it simply hasn't happened. If the hand-out from the Motor Show organisers says Press Day is from nine o'clock, then that's what the News Editor expects. You have to suppress a tendency to lose your head by telling yourself it will all be okay. And, of course, it usually is. But then again, quite often it isn't.

By half past ten the exhibition hall looked like an exhibition and not just a heap of assembled crates, and by quarter past eleven the motorbike dispatch rider was zipping back to ATV laboratories with the film, while I was slumped peacefully in the back of a cab proceeding more sedately towards the ATV studios. The film crew stayed behind to do a bit more filming at leisure, so I would have a choice of shots for the *Five Forty-Five* bulletin and *News at Ten*.

As with the majority of news stories, that one went off smoothly except for that one breathless moment at half-past eight, surveying a virtually empty exhibition hall.

I have a recurring dream, where I'm sitting at a typewriter trying to get a story together. And whatever I do, I just can't write the first sentence. Behind me I can hear that we will be on the air in thirty seconds. I know that I'm not going to make it, and the story won't be there in time.

In practice, this couldn't happen, as there are too many other people, film editors, scriptwriters and chiefs, buzzing around for anyone to get into that position.

I used to worry about this dream, till I confided it to one of my more senior colleagues.

He stared at me, for a moment. 'What, you get it too?'

## 5

### BAD NEWS

But that dream can be horribly vivid, and you dream again and again about the same stories. But the really rough ones often have innocent beginnings.

'I'm not terribly clear what we're doing here,' said the Cameraman, pulling into the side of the road. I dug myself out from a puzzled scrutiny of Bartholemews All-England Gazetteer.

'We're in Huntingdon.' About three yards ahead a large sign aggressively confirmed that statement.

'Yes,' said the Cameraman, in the tone of one humouring a three-year-old. 'But *should* we be in Huntingdon?' We all had another look at the map.

We were heading for a small village in the north of Cambridgeshire, to interview a bloke who went in for ham TV. That's right; a sort of updated version of ham radio. The TV amateurs can transmit to each other in the conventional fashion, transmitting moving pictures over short distances. But they also have a system called 'slow scan' by which they can send still pictures right round the world.

'We shouldn't be anywhere near Huntingdon,' said the Sound Recordist in disgust, squinting at the map.

Which goes to show that a grade two in geography and map reading at 'O' level is no use at all when it comes to doing anything practical.

I thankfully relinquished command of the map to the Sound Recordist and settled down to enjoy the scenery for the rest of the drive.

The camera crew travel in company Volvos, all blue, with radios to keep in touch with base. The radios only operate within the London area; beyond that it's back to the good old phone box, assuming you can find one that works. The boot of the car is packed tight with camera equipment, and the back seat jammed with anoraks, map books, the *Good Food Guide* and occasionally the Cameraman's laundry.

If there is a six-inch space left over, the reporter slots into it. Technically, the crews don't have to carry the reporters with them, but as ITN doesn't provide reporters with cars, it's usually simpler to 'go with the crew' than trust to the untender mercies of cab drivers.

I'm a great believer in the virtues of rail travel, but rail timetables seem designed to prevent you getting where you want to go until approximately this time next week.

'According to this map we're going in the wrong direction,' said the Sound Recordist, turning round to look at me accusingly. I shrugged and gave what I hoped was a pathetically winsome smile.

We cruised into a petrol station to ask directions. As the Cameraman was exchanging chit-chat with the pump attendant, a couple of ambulances tore past, closely followed by a police car.

We watched them laconically. As far as we were concerned, they could be going to pick up the bits after a minor punch-up. You don't go chasing after every ambulance you see just in case it might make news.

I bought some choccie bars in the garage shop by way of silent apology for taking the crew forty miles out of their way, and for the next ten minutes we drove along peaceably, discussing the relative merits of Crunchies, Mars Bars and Liquorice All-Sorts.

Another ambulance shot past.

'I wonder what's going on?' I said, my mouth full of Mars Bar.

'Just ten people all dialled 999 at once about the same incident,' said the Cameraman.

'Really?' I was interested. 'What happens?'

'Well,' he said, 'if there's a fire or something, sometimes they send out on each 999 call they get. So you can get fire, police *and* ambulance, when all that's happened is someone's chip pan has caught fire.'

'Nasty things, chip pans,' said the Sound Recordist, and proceeded to tell a horror story involving chip pans and curtains, and ending in total conflagration.

On cue, a fire engine went past, sirens going.

'I think,' said the Cameraman reflectively, turning on the car radio, 'we perhaps ought to listen to the news.'

'This is the World at One.' That's the BBC, always on time.

'An RAF Canberra has crashed into a row of houses at Huntingdon in Cambridgeshire.'

'Good God!' I said, shocked.

The Cameraman was slewing the car across the road, spinning back towards Huntingdon. He was an old hand, and quite unflustered.

'Keep a lookout,' he said. 'See if you can see any fire.' I scanned the countryside. We were doing about ninety on the narrow country roads. I hung on to the door handle trying to keep my balance.

I was also trying to control the mixed emotions of any reporter facing a major story, when that story is all too clearly going to involve somebody else's real tragedy. Excitement and apprehension in a confused jumble.

'There it is,' I said. A cloud of smoke hung on our left. We

81

headed towards it.

It had been just on noon when the RAF Canberra crashed into a row of houses. The police had set up a kind of back way into the housing estate across a field. We showed our Metropolitan Police press cards, which identify us as members of ITN, and were waved through. It was about a five-minute walk to the houses, but from where we stood we could see the wreckage.

'Go and phone the News Desk,' said the Cameraman to me. 'We'll start filming.'

Apart from the shattered houses, the nearest sign of a phone was about a mile back down the road we had come. The Cameraman had gone off with the car keys, so I ran out into the road and flagged down a car. The driver was a member of the local council and, luckily, one of those people for whom nothing is too much trouble.

'There are some US airforce houses just down the road,' he said. 'We'll try there.'

We drove to the nearest house, which belonged to an American airman. He and his wife let us use it as a base all day — a rendezvous for motorbike riders picking up film, and for phone messages from the office. I gave him a tenner at the end of the day; in retrospect not enough for phonecalls and lots of cups of tea. The Americans take TV crews on their doorstep in their stride.

'I'm at the crash,' I told the News Desk, the American family listening.

'Why didn't you phone me and say you were on your way there?' said the News Editor. They already had another reporter on the way, in case I hadn't heard about the crash and had gone on to my original story.

'I thought we should get here as fast as possible,' I explained. We arranged that a motorbike would pick up the film, in a couple of hours, and that I'd drive back to London to try to get something on the *Five Forty-Five* bulletin. The other reporter would stay on to pick up anything else later.

The councillor was waiting in his car to drive me back up to the crash.

A small crowd stood watching, some of them crying. The film crew were working away. 'Find some eye-witnesses,' said the Cameraman. A young man who lived directly opposite told us he was looking out of his window, and ran across as the plane hit.

A middle-aged woman called Tessa was in her house when the plane crashed into it. She had been in the kitchen and still wore her flowered apron. Now she wept as she looked at the ruin. She was stunned with shock, and still didn't realise how lucky she was to be alive.

The ground round the crash was awash with aircraft fuel. Firemen were wearing breathing apparatus because of the smoke and fumes, and two tenders had turned up from the RAF station to help. The watching crowd were telling the few reporters who'd arrived that the housing estate was directly under the flight path to the base. 'I've always been afraid something like this might happen,' said one woman.

The plane had been returning from a routine photographic mission over Scotland, and had been coming in to land at RAF Wyton two miles away, when it had gone out of control.

Five people had died when the aircraft crashed into eight terraced homes, brushing the rooftops before piling up in the front gardens, and bursting into flames.

We arrived just over an hour after it had happened. This was remarkably quick to be on the scene of such an incident; only the sheer chance of our being in the area allowed it.

The street was at one end of the estate. Another hundred yards and the aircraft would have missed it completely, crashing instead into open fields.

The police had stretched out white tapes to keep spectators back. Behind them smouldered the remains of the plane, blackened and almost unrecognisable. The roof had been swept off the terrace. The overall impression was disjointed: scattered, charred pieces of machinery, ground soaked with water and petrol, unnameable shapes wrapped in black plastic, waiting for the ambulances. A terrible smell of petrol and burning; men and women crying. And through all this the firemen moving purposefully.

A man in his fifties came up to me. 'Local paper,' he said, fishing a flask from his trenchcoat pocket. It was whisky; I swallowed some thankfully.

'Time to go, I think,' said the Cameraman, joining us for a drink of the scotch. 'We'll have to rush to get back in time for the *Five Forty-Five*.'

As we left, we saw the other crew and reporter arriving, and waved as we passed. We gave the film to the dispatch rider, who was waiting at the Americans' house, then headed for London. The film, with a bit of luck, would arrive first, so it would have time to be processed. It takes forty minutes to an hour to develop newsfilm, then it has to be edited. In contrast, the reporter's contribution, actually writing the script, takes a fraction of the time.

Back to the office, leaving a number of traffic regulations in tatters, and into the Newsroom. The *Five Forty-Five*, known as the 'Early' or 'Early bulletin', were having collective hysteria. They intended to lead on the story, and it was now quarter to five. An hour to go.

I went off into a corner and started to write. The *News at One* Producer came over to me, leaned across and whispered, 'Take a deep breath, and don't let anyone panic you. Just do it.' I did as he said and started . . .

'It was just on noon when . . .'

The story went off without a hitch. The Film Editor pulled out the best shots and best sound, with very little reference to me. I put my script round his editing — the best way to do it really. Then, because it was too late to dub (to pre-record my voice) I read over the film 'live' on air.

On *News at Ten* the film, picture and content stayed much the same, but I had to record my commentary. The other reporter on the story had done an interview with an Air Vice Marshall, but some sort of technical hitch had developed and his film was blank. So the story stayed mine.

I recorded *News at Ten*, and went up to the bar for a drink. I was beginning to get an emotional reaction.

'Don't let the bosses see you upset,' said one of the writers. He shrugged, 'They'll think women are not up to hard news.'

I thought of the black plastic bundles. 'I did it, didn't I?' I said. 'But it was just as well I had such a good cameraman.'

And went home to bed.

The problem with 'hard' stories isn't so much reporting on them. In many ways they're the easiest — the story just 'tells' itself. It's actually hanging on to the story and fighting off takeover bids that's difficult. Take the Iranian Embassy siege, where I was unequivocally outgunned and outnumbered.

I'd been having one of those quiet periods — long spells of doing the *Telegraph* crosswords, punctuated by forays to London Zoo to interview orang-utans or suchlike. Anyway, I'd decided that, if things were quiet, I might just as well catch up on my social life.

I'd no story in prospect that particular day, and was just varnishing my nails, preparatory to going out for lunch, when the News Editor zipped over.

'Iranian Embassy takeover, it's all very unclear. So and So has gone down. Would you go and see if he needs any help.' Now that's precisely the way straight to a reporter's heart — send them to help someone else.

Still, it's what pays the grocery bill so, mustering enthusiasm, I sprinted out of the Newsroom and tumbled into a cab. Down at the Embassy a large crowd of press were flattened against railings leading into a private driveway. Nobody seemed to know what was going on. I found So and So, who explained that the Embassy had been taken over, and the policeman on duty outside had been taken over with it. He didn't want to leave the site to talk to *News at One*, so I trotted off to find a phone.

*News at One* wanted a 'phono', that's to say a phone-call, saying what was going on. I had only the shakiest idea, but I gathered that was as much as anyone else had.

I went into a block of flats and asked the porter if I could use the payphone. 'Sure,' he said. Unfortunately, when I was just embarked on a 'live' phone call into the programme, the porter opened the call-box door.

'You'll have to get off that phone,' he said. 'One of the residents wants to use it.' He had that satisfied expression a certain type of man wears when they're being difficult.

Fortunately for me, the door opened inwards, so I put my full weight against it and held him outside while I raced through my story for *News at One*.

No one who has not done a live phone call on the news, while holding a door, glass at that, which is being pounded by an irate porter, can quite imagine the sensation. When someone later complained that I had spoken too quickly, I thought of explaining, but somehow couldn't summon the energy.

Back at the Embassy the police had corralled the press behind metal barriers a good couple of hundred yards from the scene of excitement. Our outside broadcast unit had arrived and were busily chatting up a top cop. The OB director seemed to have immediately struck up a great rapport with the boys in blue, and had got all our OB vans nice and close to the barrier.

The News Desk told me to stay down and help So and So for the rest of the day, which was mostly spent eyeing the Embassy from a distance and wondering what would happen next. ITN sent down a sheaf of sandwiches and coffee, which we had to guard against predatory raids from the press. One of the American networks was busy setting up a scaffolding tower to give themselves a good view. Our OB director had imported a crane, which raised the camera fifty feet in the air, giving a marvellous outlook.

For *News at Ten*, my colleague went back to do a long film package, detailing the events of the day, while I did two on-the-spot reports live from the outside broadcast cameras. I went home that night after handing over to the unfortunate who had to do the all-night watch, in a state of high elation. It looked like I'd tagged on to a good story. Alas, next day, after *News at One*, I was hauled back to the office.

'Why?' I bleated to the Deputy Editor.

'You can't do it all,' he said.

'Why not?' I asked in injured tones.

He ignored that and retired purposefully behind a stack of paperwork. His voice drifted from under a pile of memos.

'Why don't you go and get some sleep?'

They kept So and So on the story, but changed the OB reporter each day. When the whole thing was over, and the Embassy blown up, the office decided to keep a watch all the next night, presumably in case someone tried to pinch the wreckage. I drew the short straw.

BBC radio, the *Evening Standard* and self spent a gloomy night huddled inside an ITN van. We rationed out tea from a vacuum flask like three refugees.

'I wish I knew what I was doing here,' said the *Evening Standard*, a plump and peachy woman not given to losing her cool.

She disposed herself on the floor, covered herself with her coat and put her granny glasses carefully on the floor.

'Wake me up if anything happens.'

A moment later she was out cold. The BBC followed her example.

I did the *Telegraph* crossword. I had nine hours to do it in, and I still couldn't finish it. I just wanted to go to sleep.

'Well,' said Julie. 'That's the glamorous TV life for you. You should settle for a peaceful routine like mine.'

She'd come round to see me next day as the Boyfriend, having discussed the etymology of the English language with her very satisfactorily for the past couple of months, had gone off to lecture in the States for a fortnight. This seemed a good opportunity to try and retrieve my best evening dress to which Julie appeared to have staked a claim. One thing her Rio experiences had taught her was that possession was nine and nine-tenths points of the law.

'About my Chinese dress,' I said optimistically.

'Yes, you are sweet,' said she. 'I've got this dinner party tomorrow. You're so kind. I'm going with a smashing feller.'

'Another one,' I yelped, feeling that Someone Up There was getting fair shares badly out of balance. 'What does he do?'

'He's an endocrinologist,' she said with a dopey smile. I briefly contemplated discovering precisely what an endocrinologist was, but reckoned that she'd have moved on to pastures new before I'd managed to find it in the dictionary.

'I'm exhausted,' I said. We'd just been watching my efforts on the news.

'I don't know why,' said Julie. 'All you've done is hang around Kensington for a couple of days. I can't think why they pay you.'

I ignored that. 'I want my dress back,' I said, changing the subject abruptly.

'I thought you said you were going to sleep all weekend?'

'Yes,' I said cautiously.

'Well, you won't need it. Can I have it for another week?'

'A week? The dinner's tomorrow.'

She gave one of those bland smiles which cause strong men to turn faint and trembling.

'There's a sort of dance next Friday, at the University.'

'The endocrinologist?' I asked wearily.

'Oh no, just a physicist.'

'What about Michael?' Michael being the unfortunate currently in the States.

'He wouldn't want me to sit and mope. Anyway, I bet *he* isn't doing much moping. I know what the American lecture circuit's like.'

She always was unduly cynical.

# 6

## DO NOT ADJUST YOUR SET

I can be quite cynical myself at times, and the most profound conviction I've developed about TV and TV technology is that any camera more complicated than a Kodak Brownie is a delusion, a mockery and a snare. There's a kind of sub-theme running through a reporter's life: anything that can break down will, usually at the most inconvenient moment and on a day when the gadget needed to fix it has somehow been left behind at the office.

It doesn't just apply to cameras. There are horrific stories remembered over drinks in the small hours, of exploding lights, steaming photocopiers, and typewriters that bite back.

Hard-bitten veterans of a dozen wars tremble with emotion as they recall exclusive interviews which, when processed, produced only blank film. Their voices shake as they describe trying to satellite film from remote parts of the world where the local TV engineers have never used satellite equipment before and are reading from their instruction book, with the help of a Spanish-English dictionary, whilst they try to transmit the precious story. Even on the most mundane level the mechanical world conspires against you.

Perhaps we treat machines too casually and they don't like it. For instance, the TV Newsroom is plastered wall to wall with TV sets, known in the trade as 'monitors'. These are mainly used for watching the news on the other channel, just to make sure we haven't missed anything. The sets, of course, can be employed for less innocent activities, switching through to the studio, for example, to watch some hopeful type's camera test.

Well, these monitors are always breaking down, usually in the last ten minutes of the late-night movie, just when the fellow's about to take off the girl's clothes. One night, right in the middle of a Bond film — that bit somewhere between the second girl and the third assassination — the set flickered and died. So we called one of the 'vision maintenance' engineers (sounds like an optician) to fix it.

He arrived, clearly annoyed at being dragged away from watching the same film on his set. He looked at the TV, fixed on a bracket high up on the wall. Then he stood on a chair and thumped it. Hard. The set flickered, the picture reappeared in black and white. He thumped it again. The screen coloured. Perfect.

'Mechanical shock,' said the engineer as he stumped off. 'Works even better if you kick it.'

It was somewhere around this point that I realised the human intellect has never really got over the shock of inventing the wheel.

But you can't kick TV film cameras. Or at least, it's inadvisable. For a start, they cost about eight thousand pounds, and violence doesn't do them any good at all. But there are moments when my foot positively itches as I stand trying to make light conversation with an interviewee while the entire film crew stare in a puzzled way at the entrails of a camera that has just sighed to a standstill.

There was a time I interviewed the head of the BBC World Service. This was just after an election, when the new government were scything through public spending with all the enthusiasm of a new broom that finds itself armed with bayonets instead of bristles. It looked as if the World Service was about to suffer considerable and painful amputation, so I trotted along to find out how our colleagues at the Beeb were taking the matter.

Now if there is one occasion above all others when you wash your face and wipe your feet, it's when trampling all over the opposition's best carpets. So, all on our best behaviour, we toddled down to Bush House in the Strand where the World Service operates.

The World Service transmits to the wind's four quarters, or thereabouts. You can call it keeping the flag flying or filthy capitalist propaganda, depending on whether you favour blue ties or pink, but whatever they're up to, they certainly make a good job of it.

The building has an imposing white façade, but inside it's very scruffy and shows the effects of successive cutbacks in spending. All the cash goes on the service and not on the paintwork. Because the service is directed at foreign countries, not the home market, they don't get a lot of publicity. In fact, the threatened cuts had turned the home spotlight full on, rather to their advantage, as all the quality press were running articles saying how the World Service in English was well worth listening to.

My camera team gazed in some awe at recording equipment which took them back to their shadowy youth. I couldn't make head or tail of it; vast spools of tape in enormous cabinets with thirties-style veneer.

'What do you mean, "thirties style"?' said my Sound Recordist, examining the equipment closely. 'It's *genuine* thirties. This stuff's all of fifty years old.'

So it was with considerable awe that we continued our tour. The Newsroom is much like Newsrooms anywhere else — lots of desks jammed together with lots of people giving the appearance of doing a lot of work. Just off the Newsroom is a small studio where the English-language news is read. This is transmitted just about all over the world, and you can hear it at home too, if you tune to World Service on M/W 648 kHz (463m).

This studio is totally modern. But the newsreader speaks much more slowly than on home radio or TV, and there seem to be plenty of people who think it sounds better.

First of all there are a few bars of *Lillibulero* and then the time signal. The newsreader says, 'This is the BBC World Service,' and proceeds to read the news carefully and evenly.

Every so often during the bulletin, at random intervals, the reader repeats, 'This is the BBC World Service'; that's to stop any nasty, sneaky, foreign radio stations from pinching the news and re-transmitting it as their own.

After we'd filmed the real news broadcast, we got them to play the tape of *Lillibulero* and the time signal a few times, so that we could get a good clear recording. Then we interviewed the boss on how he felt about the financial axe whistling round his ears.

I was a bit nervous about doing this interview. I mean, I might need a job at the Beeb some day. But anyway, we all trooped into his big office — shabby, like the rest of the building — and shook hands.

The interview went off smoothly enough, apart from the fact that I suddenly had a complete mental blackout and forgot his name, so compromised by calling him 'Sir' every other sentence. The interview went on for far too long, as it was a bit difficult to wind it up. Eventually we shook hands again and were preparing to depart when the Cameraman looked closely at his camera and stiffened. Then he fixed me with the sort of expression a subaltern might have worn before going over the top.

'Could I possibly have a quick word?' It's a bad sign when people are far too polite.

'We'll have to do the interview again,' he muttered. 'The battery's flat.'

TV film cameras are electrically driven. They have a special rechargeable battery, not at all like the thing you put in a tranny, so a flat battery is a fairly routine hazard.

I crawled back to the World Service boss and made a fairly good job of trying to hide under the carpet as I explained that we were going to have to do an action replay. This was especially embarassing, as he'd just been saying he was in rather a hurry to get away. He was very civil about it, and we did the interview all over again. But I hope I never have to apply to him for a job.

Outside, the Cameraman, now back to his usual breezy self, asked, 'What did you apologise so much for? These things will happen.'

'Sure,' said I, 'but did it have to happen at the BBC?'

Well, the saga doesn't end there. To try and give a fresh angle on the threatened cuts at the World Service I'd arranged to interview a Soviet journalist working in London as correspondent for *Novosti*. The Soviet Embassy press office had refused an interview with any official Embassy staff, but had suggested this man instead. We could still be sure he would be giving the official line. It wasn't that we didn't know exactly how the USSR felt about the service, but it sounds better getting a Russian to say it than me.

The Russian and his wife lived in a smart block of flats just off Kensington High Street. A really good capitalist address in fact. The only other person I know who lives in that vicinity is the boss of a travel firm who's filthy rich.

They had a smart flat, slightly underfurnished in a rather chic way, and the only real sign that it was anything other than a well-to-do English home was a photo of Lenin on the bookcase. The journalist's wife presented us with glasses of vodka. It was nine in the morning.

After this muscular breakfast, we duly recorded the interview in which the Russian told us, in excellent English, how the BBC were broadcasting propaganda, and I asked well, what about Radio Moscow then? And a lot more of the same.

Then there was more handshaking all round; the elegant wife asked me where I bought my dress; we declined more vodka emphatically; and drove with extreme caution back to the office. Though, as the Cameraman said, 'Who's even going to imagine breathalysing us at this hour?'

In the Newsroom I wrote a commentary which tried to express how wonderful the World Service was without sounding too much as if I wanted a job there. The Russian's interview turned out very well, and I thought was going to do no harm at all to his promotion chances.

Just as we were about to go on the air for *News at One* came the ultimate hitch, the one besides which all others fade away. Technicians in the London area went into dispute and we were blacked out. I imagine the Soviets felt that proved their point. I just hope the boss of the BBC World Service wasn't sitting waiting to see himself on the box. He'd have died laughing.

Flat batteries do happen at the most dreadful moments. It happened, yet again, when I was attempting to interview Spike Milligan. He was speaking at a demonstration against the slaughter of baby seals, and we conducted the interview in the middle of an interested crowd of about five hundred people, with a woman in the background waving a fluffy toy seal on a pole.

'Toy Town TV,' said Spike when I explained we'd have to do it again.

But he did it, and in fact it was a rather better interview the second time, with a nice quotable quote about rich women going into hotels wearing dead animals around their shoulders. I'd been thinking vaguely about investing in a secondhand fur coat, but rather went off the idea after that.

The real camera killer is cold weather. When the temperature drops, there's a greatly increased chance that the camera will seize up. This is partly because of the way the film is wound on, held on top of the camera in a detachable 'magazine', 'mag' for short. It's rather as if the cartridge on an ordinary camera was outside instead of inside. And, unlike a cartridge, the film mag is emptied and reloaded by the cameraman. On location he does this using a black bag with sleeves for his hands — a sort of portable darkroom. The film is wound through the mag by a pulley system that hoicks the film past the lens. This pulley is on the outside, and when it's cold and wet has a nasty tendency to stick. It does seem to be cold and wet for a substantial chunk of the British summer. But it's not fair to blame the camera for everything; there are even more delicious horrors.

It was the deep midwinter, as the carol puts it. And snow on snow had been falling determinedly all night. I was standing in as the News Editor on the lunch-time news, the full-time News Editor having rather sensibly developed a nasty cough was looking set to see out the freeze tucked up in bed with a hot toddy and a good book.

As I struggled out of my bed at six o'clock, the cold and damp in my flat hit me like a lungful of icecream. The central heating storage radiators seemed to make no impact at all. I tried to clean my chattering teeth while listening, moderately aghast, to the news. The entire country seemed to be snowed up, and a crowd of schoolchildren in Yorkshire hadn't even been able to get home for the night and had had to sleep in school.

Now, this was the sort of story that jumped up and hit you in the face begging to be noticed. It was essential to get up to the school quickly, before the kids were all out of their makeshift beds and rescued by snowplough. But the snow, the snow. If the children couldn't get home, we were going to have a spot of trouble getting to them.

The TV company that operates in that area has a helicopter. But helicopters are expensive. At seven o'clock in the morning there was no one else in the office to ask for advice, and I have an inbuilt aversion to disturbing people at home unless absolutely necessary. We're always being told to use our initiative, so I dusted off mine and got into action.

I booked the helicopter. Then phoned a reporter who was in the area on another story and diverted him and his crew to catch the whirlybird. Just to be on the safe side, I sent another cameraman along as well. Those snowed-up children wouldn't know what had hit them.

Sitting at the News Desk you tend to get a rather detached view of events. The news comes to you pasteurised, as it were, through phone messages. Twenty-foot snow drifts where reporter, cameraman and sound recordist are trying to dig out the car decode as 'The film will be an hour late'. Demonstrations in Hyde Park translate as 'Use a dispatch rider to get the film through the traffic', and a bomb blast means the camera crew will have trouble finding somewhere to park.

On this particular day all the messages were coming through nice and easy. True, I had temporarily lost a cameraman who'd gone to film snowdrifts in Sussex, and was probably now buried beneath one, but that was a minor worry.

Most importantly, the reporter who had gone to the school had done his filming and was heading back to the local TV station in good time to have his stuff ready for one o'clock.

The various TV companies throughout Britain can link up by a system of 'lines' which carry sound and picture. The story comes down a line and is recorded on videotape, then it's re-transmitted in the news. Sending a story like this is quite complicated. The reporter has to go to a regional TV studio where his film is processed in the laboratories, then edited before the electronic wizardry takes over and it's sent to London.

The phone rang; the film had arrived at the studios and was being processed. All was going well.

It was some forty minutes before I heard anything further. It was the regional News Editor. He sounded a shade strained. 'You are not', he said, 'going to like this.'

'What's happened?' I almost whispered down the phone.

The Producer was sitting just behind me, and there was no sense spoiling his peace until it became absolutely necessary. There was a long pause on the phone. I was conscious of the Producer, sleeves rolled up, happily finalising his plans for the programme in pleasant confidence that he had a good story coming in.

'You know that film?' asked the regional man, somewhat redundantly.

'Go on.'

'Well, it arrived here by motorbike dispatch rider and went on to labs. And well then, love, you know we've got a lot of snow up here?'

'Yes, I did have just an idea you might have.' I thought I was keeping my cool rather well.

He suddenly came to the point. 'The snow blocked all the air vents from the lab. It's full of chemical fumes and we've had to take the lab staff to hospital. I'm sorry about your film.'

'I'm sorry about your staff,' I replied, forcing the words out in a throttled squeak. He rang off hastily.

I tore my hair in a muted sort of fashion and proceeded to relate events to the Producer. In the circumstances, he took it remarkably well.

'It can't be helped,' he said. But for the rest of the morning I could hear his teeth grinding gently in the background.

When I finally got home that night, it was with the certain knowledge that I'd caught the News Editor's flu. I was streaming

96

with sweat but, even so, the chill in my flat seeped into my chest. I touched the storage heaters. They were faintly warm. I went into the kitchen and lit all the gas rings, lit the oven and left its door open. I was fairly hungry as I'd been working for six days without a break, and the fridge contained one egg and some pineapple-flavoured cottage cheese, neither of which looked remotely interesting. I phoned Julie and appealed for help. Then I went to bed.

Julie arrived, laden with cans of soup and a bottle of brandy. Hot tomato soup and brandy is a lovely cold cure.

She sneered at the radiators. 'Why,' she asked, with devastating logic, 'don't you fork out twenty pounds for a decent convector heater?'

As she was sitting on the end of my bed with a blanket draped around her shoulders over her coat, warming her hands on the soup mug, with the radiators full on and an electricity bill of a hundred pounds a quarter, I agreed she probably had a point.

She leaned over and pressed her hand to the wall plaster. It left a soggy indentation. 'What this flat needs is a damp course.'

I shivered under my duvet and thought of a new heater.

There was a bewildering range of convector heaters on show when I tottered down to the supermarket, still sniffing and leaving a trail of paper hankies in my wake.

The supermarket was one of those which, having for the past umpteen years confined their activities decently to selling baked beans and fish fingers, have now expanded into heat resistant ovenware, portable TVs and gadgets for crushing garlic. In the midst of all this was a little flock of electric heaters. As I don't know anything about things electrical, I used the wine-ordering technique: always choose the second cheapest. The second cheapest heater was an inoffensive-looking model in grey metal with a grille at the front. There were three switches on the top to vary the temperature between, I hoped, warm, very warm and tropical. I duly paid for the device and staggered back to my flat, revelling in the thought of basking in heat.

It was only when I got home that I realised it didn't have a plug. And the only plug in the flat was firmly attached to the TV set. It was a close shave between the late film and the heater, but in the end I wrapped myself up in the duvet and shivered throughout the evening, eyeing the offending heater balefully whenever the plot dragged.

At last the whole thing was nicely wired up and I gloated at the walls positively steaming with heat.

I rang Julie and offered reciprocal hospitality for the soup, and suggested she might like to admire the heater.

'It's lovely and warm,' she said, 'but what's the smell of burning plastic?' she added thoughtfully.

I couldn't smell any burning plastic, but that could have been because of my cold.

Some hours later, after a dissertation on the virtues of the latest man, Julie went off home full of braised steak, Beaujolais and the remains of the brandy.

Then I began to think I could smell burning myself. I looked round in confusion, my disorientation assisted by the effects of dinner, and was just deciding that I really must lay off the booze when I saw a small flame emanating from the plug behind the heater.

They do say that all women carry within them the sense of racial preservation. I don't know about that, but within twenty seconds I'd disconnected the electricity at the mains and was smothering the fire with a fire blanket I'd borrowed as a student and never returned. As I surveyed the blackened wall, it crossed my mind that all the technical trouble I seem to run into at work might be because I've a bad aura or something. Machines have definitely got it in for me.

I was so full of wrath at the thought of being barbecued in my sleep that next day I headed back to the supermarket, the remains of the heater under my arm.

'I want to see the manager, please.'

The assistant eyed me with anaemic alarm, biting her lip and obviously thinking I was from the VAT or something.

I displayed the heater. The three-pin plug had melted, a miserable little lump of charred plastic with its three metal prongs sticking stiffly out like legs on a dead cockroach.

'Oh,' said the assistant. She took another look, holding the plug close to myopic eyes. 'Golly,' she continued, rather inadequately, I thought. I had employed stronger language myself.

She wiped her hands down her blue check overall and went to summon help.

The manager was one of those weedy little men who wear equally weedy little moustaches just to prove they can. In his case this was most definitely a bad idea, as his facial hair was completely outclassed by the luxuriant growth of his senior assistant, a lady of mature years and formidable figure. She looked at me as if I were a very small mouse and she a rather hungry cat. I wouldn't have liked to argue with her. But the manager was determined to handle the matter himself. That was his first mistake.

'So, what have we got here?' He picked up the heater, turned it over in his hands and put it down again. 'It looks all right to me.'

I gestured speechlessly at the blackened plug which he had overlooked. He lifted the charred blob and examined it judicially, then he snapped his fingers. The moustached lady handed him a screwdriver. With some difficulty he undid what remained of the plug and inspected the wiring. He stroked his wispy moustache.

'Well, the wiring looks okay,' he said, in what he presumably imagined were impressive tones. 'Did your husband do it?'

'No, I did it,' I replied. Well, this was the truth, and I really rather resent anyone assuming I can't so much as wire a plug.

'Oh, dear,' he said and shook his head. Then he 'Oh, deared' a bit more.

'You really shouldn't have, love. Couldn't you have got your boyfriend to do it? Very tricky to mess around with electrical things. Oh, dear.'

I thought this showed a certain touching faith that the days of chivalry had not passed. I find blokes who're expected to double as handymen rapidly vanish from the scene.

However, ignoring this diversion, I replied, 'But you said the wiring looked okay.'

He shook his head mournfully. The moustached lady shook her head too. I glared at her. The manager then began busily to employ the screwdriver, fitting a new plug. Now, working with TV gear has installed in me a great respect for all things electric — especially when they're playing up.

'Don't you think', I asked, 'that you ought to get the store's electrician?'

'Are you implying', he said, 'that I can't wire a plug?'

Well, of course, that was exactly what I was doing. He carried

99

on fitting the new plug while I watched warily.

'Look,' I said finally, my sadistic desire to see him electrocuted overcome by some atavistic emotion of decency. 'There really is something very wrong with that heater. Honestly, I wouldn't plug it in if I were you.'

'I know what I'm doing, and I'll thank you not to tell me my job,' was all I got for that.

By now there was quite a cluster of interested customers and shop assistants standing around watching the performance. The manager shook his head at them.

'She wired the plug up wrongly, and now comes in here wanting her money back.' He moved to push the plug into a socket.

At that I backed away behind a six-foot stack of baked bean cans. I was rather gratified to see that the assembled shoppers, and indeed the shop assistants as well, were also moving out of the way. After all, most housewives change plugs as a matter of everyday routine, and they were showing considerably more reliance on my word than on the manager's. The moustached lady was also beginning to look a bit unhappy and retired behind a rack of condensed soup. The whole shop fell quiet as we waited to see what would happen.

The manager pushed the plug into the point. Nothing happened. He switched on the heater. It buzzed away happily, working perfectly. Still nothing happened. Hidden behind the baked bean tins, I began to get a horrible sinking feeling that, after all, I had wired up the plug the wrong way. I peeked round the tins and eyed the manager.

'You see,' he said. 'Works perfectly.'

At that moment, right on cue, there was a most morally satisfying bang and flash, and all the lights went out. We stood there in the dark and looked at each other. The supermarket was lit only by the glow from a fridge which must have been on another circuit. I felt that this really was the moment to make my excuses and leave, but I still wanted my cash back. The manager scowled at me.

'Give madam her money back.' His voice squeaked with anger.

The shop assistants were shaking with laughter. As I went to the till to collect the loot, the moustached lady winked at me, which goes to show there's good in everyone.

I heard later that the shop had lost several hundred pounds of goods in shoplifting during the blackout, although even I hardly felt I could ask the manager to confirm that.

I was faintly embarrassed about the whole business, and for a few weeks used another shop. But that supermarket was handy and really quite good, so I decided to go back and just stare the manager out if he said anything.

But I needn't have worried. I don't know what happened, but I never saw him again. The new manager was really nice and always smiled and said hello. And then, when I bought an electric toaster, he made a special point of putting the plug on for me himself.

So what with exploding heaters and disintegrating cameras, I've tended not to trust my luck with machines. They've undeniably got minds of their own. And I decided that to run my own car round London would be laying the red carpet down and inviting trouble to walk right up it. I take cabs in the fond expectation that other people's gadgets might be immune. Some hope. . . .

# 7

## DIRTY WORK

The minicab engine clunked. Then it clunked again. It was a persistent and aggressive sort of noise, rather as if someone had left a couple of tin cans under the bonnet.

I looked at the minicab driver and he looked at me. Then he got out of the car and looked under the bonnet. His movements were slow and cautious, as if they cost him money.

'Well?' I asked. You can get an awful lot into a 'Well' with enough practice. It's a word I find very useful when talking to minicab drivers at half past six in the morning.

'There's something wrong here,' the driver said, with great deliberation, as if he'd come to this conclusion all by himself. He turned on the engine again and fiddled hopefully with the gears. There was another clunk. 'Definitely something wrong,' he repeated, as if delivering himself of the wisdom of ages.

I groaned. 'I have to be on location in half an hour.'

The driver shrugged, then relented slightly.

'Well, I'll try.' He spoke as if he were doing me a great personal favour.

We clunked off down the road, waking the few neighbours who hadn't already been disturbed by the noise. Never buy a house next door to a journalist. It's not the late-night parties you have to worry about, it's the dawn alarms. This particular minicab firm used to send a man who hooted his horn outside the front door instead of knocking. He once did this at four o'clock in the morning. My next-door neighbour didn't speak to me for a month.

The car now seemed to be going okay despite the noise and a slight smell of burning. I retired behind the *Daily Mirror* in what I hoped was a truly dreadful silence. It was a half-hour drive to the location, and I'd progressed through the *Mirror* and *Mail* and was now on the *Telegraph*, as the engine sighed to a death rattle.

'It's near here somewhere,' said the driver, looking at me hopefully.

I repeated the address. He took out a street map with an injured air. I returned to the *Telegraph* crossword. After going round the square twice and then the wrong way up a one-way street, waking half London in the process, we finally arrived.

A clutch of press cars showed that this was the right place. My camera crew were there too, leaning on their car. I signed the minicab bill and the driver left noisily, clunking off to wake any who'd survived the initial assault.

This was 'D' day in the Anthony Blunt affair — the day he was giving his interviews. ITN didn't know where he had been staying the night before, so had sent me to lurk outside his solicitor's house, just in case. Quite a lot of other people seemed to have had the same idea, which only goes to show how unimaginative News Editors are as a breed. Every under-employed hack from Fleet

Street was propping up the garden fence and admiring the rose bushes.

The *Standard* strolled over, shivering in an inadequately lightweight mac.

'He's not here.'

He didn't need to say who. Another couple of pressmen wandered up to see if I knew anything they didn't. Then we all stood and shivered and they smoked each other's cigarettes while I hit the chewing-gum, and we all tried to see if anyone was looking at us through the net curtains.

'Has anyone knocked on the door?' I asked.

The others looked at me and then ostentatiously at their watches. It was still only seven o'clock.

'He really isn't here?' I tried to sound as if I only wanted to be reassured.

'No, we think he's with a boyfriend,' said the *Standard*, softening slightly.

'What about his solicitor?'

'We think he's left already.'

'There's a light on in the kitchen,' said someone I didn't know.

That is what News Editors call 'investigative reporting'.

'It'll be Mrs Solicitor getting the kids up,' said someone else.

This is what News Editors call 'letting the facts spoil a good story'.

Then Mrs Solicitor did indeed emerge. She smiled charmingly at us all and promised that her husband wasn't in the house. What about Professor Blunt? She laughed and told us he wasn't there either. Then she whisked off, leaving a little puddle of reporters wondering what their respective News Desks would think up for them to do next.

An hour later, we had all migrated south and were renewing our lurk outside *The Times*. Originally, Professor Blunt had been thought to be giving a press conference at ITN but, for reasons I know nothing about, the venue had been switched to 'The Thunderer'. Indeed, the location was supposed to be secret, but *The Times* had clearly been leaking like a colander.

The same small mob who had collected outside the solicitor's home were now reinforced by several dozen late risers, plus a twitter of TV crews.

ITN, the BBC and *The Times* were going to be allowed to interview Mr Blunt, and perhaps even ask him just the odd tiny awkward question. A reporter from the Press Association was to be allowed to take notes, and the rest of Fleet Street would have to make do with that.

It was an unbelievable situation. The Prime Minister wouldn't get away with making conditions like that.

ITN was to have one reporter inside doing the interview and me, plus two others, outside. The reporter who was actually going to quiz Blunt now showed up all keen and enthusiastic. Well, he hadn't been struggling with minicabs at half past six. This charmer, a youth with a taste for clipboards and flashy anoraks with shoulder pads, is known to his colleagues as Clark Kent; Superman in plain clothes.

'We've all been up since half past six,' I announced loudly. 'Someone' — looking hopefully at Clark Kent — 'someone could go and find some coffee and bacon sandwiches.'

'Great idea,' said Clark. 'Just coffee for me. I've had breakfast.'

See why he's called Clark Kent?

Defeated, I trotted off to find a sandwich bar. I bought coffee for the BBC crew as well. They were all six-footers, and coffee might make them a bit less likely to trample me in the rush if Blunt appeared. Or, once trampled, might make them less likely to jump up and down.

Blunt was allegedly due to arrive at ten o'clock. By then there were about a hundred reporters and photographers massed around *The Times*'s entrance. *The Times* hadn't been back long since its closure, and staff arriving for work looked at us in horror, thinking the paper was about to shut up shop again.

There was a noticeable amount of ill-feeling among those papers that hadn't been admitted to the press conference, and people kept dragging me off into corners to tell me what a rotten lot my employers were. 'The Thunderer' was re-christened 'The Squeak' by some who felt life and liberty were not being upheld by its role in this operation.

In between the complaints, the more tired, elderly or hungover just watched the door glassily. The younger, more enthusiastic and naive, cruised around the building trying to spot likely entrances where Blunt might arrive. Despite the massed hordes of reporters, the only people who did see Blunt were two horrible children who spotted him going through a back door. They expected a tip from the press; they don't know how lucky they were not to get thumped.

Two minutes later, Clark Kent, warmly ensconced in the interview room, radioed to me on our two-way that Blunt had indeed arrived. The horrible children, still hanging around, smirked at each other. A policeman, sensing violence in the air, moved in and chased them away.

'Stop bothering the ladies and gentlemen.'

They left sulkily.

So now we were staking out, waiting for Blunt to leave. We waited. And waited. People got bored and drifted off. The crowd thinned still further when the pubs opened. Lots of little deals were being done: 'Well, if I go for half an hour and you cover for me, then you can go for half an hour next . . .' Everyone, of course, would swear eternally to the News Desk that they'd never budged: 'Been there all day, Sam! I tell you, not a bite to eat, no cigarettes either. Dreadful day — can I have tomorrow off?'

The next news was that Blunt was having lunch in the building. This went down very badly indeed, especially among the six-thirty mob. Tomorrow's front-page stories were being written in people's heads and getting nastier by the minute.

'And he got malt whisky,' said the *News* with barely suppressed fury and a strong accent on 'malt', before going off to phone his copy. I rather looked forward to reading it.

Next, Clark Kent emerged, confirmed that Blunt was indeed having lunch, and went off to eat his.

We were all freezing cold by this time, but one of the foreign TV reporters, inspired perhaps by news of Blunt's potations, pushed off and returned with a bottle of brandy. At the same time a car drew up from ITN. The News Desk, for once alert to the disaster potential of three starving reporters plus four starving film crews, had dispatched a load of coffee and sandwiches. We traded cheese sandwiches and coffee for a shot of Courvoisier — well, several shots of Courvoisier.

Although ITN had been awarded one of the interviews, we had no idea how Blunt was going to leave, and it was a matter of some importance to the News Desk that we got a shot of his exit.

Although we were all being matey and trying to look casual, we had got the building very well covered.

*The Times* faces Gray's Inn Road. A narrow street runs between it and its sister paper, *The Sunday Times*, while the two are joined by an overhead bridge. Behind both papers runs a quiet road. Further along is a bank, and the exit to *The Times*'s underground car park. So, we not only had to watch the front and back of *The Times*, we also needed to keep an eye on *The Sunday Times*, as Blunt could be taken over the bridge, and also on the underground car park.

I was at the front of the building, watching the main door, plus the front exit of the car park, and keeping the extra eye I usually don't mention on the front of *The Sunday Times*.

Another senior reporter was baby-sitting a white Land-Rover parked at the back. We suspected this was how Blunt had arrived, as a friend of his owned just such a vehicle. Yet another hack was watching the back of *The Sunday Times*, while a camera crew, without a reporter, were staked out at the top of the car park. We also had three dispatch riders on motorbikes, all armed with two-way radios, ready for hot pursuit.

I had a faint sense of over-kill as I trotted round, a cheese sandwich in one hand and spiked coffee in the other, surveying these preparations. It may have been the brandy, but an uneasy thought struggled to the surface.

'Does anyone know,' I asked of the press at large, 'if *The Times* has a chopper pad on the roof?'

No one answered.

The preparations for Blunt's departure turned out to be so lavish that a helicopter would probably have been cheaper.

Just after three o'clock, a man dived into the white Land-Rover and tore round to the front of the building, pursued by the reporter, the crew and a dispatch rider. The Land-Rover stopped at the front entrance, throwing its pursuers into total disarray as they fell over each other. Within minutes, a red Marina drove from the underground car park with someone hiding rather conspicuously under a blanket in the back. This was a bit too good to be true and, sure enough, it was a hoax.

Into the middle of all these fun and games walked Mr Edward Heath, who had been at *The Times* for reasons quite unconnected with Blunt. He walked out of the front entrance to be almost lifted off his feet by the surge of press. He seemed to be enjoying himself and played up to the reporters who, by now, were getting rather giggly, what with the cold and the Courvoisier, and were ready for some fun.

'Are you the mole?' yelled someone. I wish it had been me. So now people were chasing white Land-Rovers, red Marinas, and Ted Heath. A few cynics stood at a slight distance from the rest of us and surveyed the pandemonium coolly. This is usually a mistake for a reporter. The Newsroom motto is: 'If you are keeping your head when all around are losing theirs, you're the only one who doesn't know what's going on.'

All this time, the real getaway car, another red Marina, had been parked unobtrusively round a corner minding its own business. By now, most of the reporters had been lured well away, except for our number three man, who had been watching the back of *The Sunday Times* and feeling rather out of it. He was chatting to a dispatch rider, when they suddenly spotted Blunt coming out the back of *The Times* thirty yards up the road. They promptly gave chase, alerting us through the motorola. There was no hiding under blankets for Mr Blunt. Oh no! He sat upright in the back seat while cameramen hung insecurely out of car windows filming him.

I'd been at the wrong side of the building, getting my tuppence-worth out of Ted Heath, so by the time I struggled out of the heaving mass of reporters and then struggled back to retrieve my right shoe, which had somehow got disconnected from the rest of me, we were well behind. I called the News Desk on the radio.

'Bet you a quid he goes to his flat,' they said.

We cut round and headed there — but he beat us to it.

The Marina drew up outside the block, a vast complex called Portsea Hall. Blunt had to face just a moment of vulgar unpleasantness as he walked the few yards to his door. There were two TV crews and about a dozen reporters, who chased round him firing questions. He didn't answer, ignored them utterly. One creep, possibly thinking sympathy would do the trick, asked, 'Did you have a very bad day, Sir Anthony?'

No answer.

Then he was inside the flats with the uniformed porter touching his cap and 'Sir Anthonying' for all he was worth. You'd never think his knighthood had been taken away. There was just a glimpse of him as he walked through the expensively carpeted hall, glittering with crystal candelabra. Then the door was barred and a policeman stood solidly in front of it.

Back at ITN there were a lot of assorted snippets of film to put together. Although a small army of ITN reporters had been chasing Blunt, I was to pull all their film together and write and voice the commentary. It was a rare chance to indulge in a little dead-pan humour. I was amused to read in one of the Sunday papers that ITN had carried a description of the 'Keystone Cops' activities. Praise, sweet praise.

But it had all been a bit too easy, or at least that's clearly what the News Desk thought. The decision was that we would stake out the flats to see if Blunt would leave. As I had done the story, I was clearly in the direct line of fire to do most of the staking out.

You would never, in a million years, have thought that Anthony Blunt was a self-confessed traitor getting away scot-free, by the way the other residents of that block of luxury flats reacted to the press. Every other one who walked past the cluster of bored, cold and increasingly irritated flock of reporters made remarks like: 'Haven't you anything better to do?' And even: 'Why don't you leave the poor man alone?'

This sort of pleasantry was producing an alarmingly right-wing spirit among the normally fairly liberal press boys and girls working on the story. I could feel my own politics shifting perceptibly towards the 'Hanging is too good for him' spectrum.

Portsea Hall is in a street just off the posh end of the Edgware Road. There's a courtyard in front which is private property, so reporters had to stand on the pavement well back from the flats. A policeman and policewoman stood in front of the block to stop us making a nuisance of ourselves.

My camera crew sprawled in the company Volvo, a picture of total gloom. The floor of the car was littered with wrappings from the nearby McDonald's.

'We've got to try and get in there,' said I, all bright-eyed and bushy-tailed.

The cameraman regarded me sadly.

'You just look at that lot of hard boys out there. If they can't get into the block, you won't.'

I looked. The *Daily Mail* was sitting on a wall drinking Pils. So was the lady from the *Standard*. The *Express* was asleep in his car. The *Daily Telegraph*'s more respectable-looking representative, a very pleasant and dapper bloke in a smart overcoat, was gazing into the sky, instantly identifiable as one struggling, but determined, to wait till opening time. This is the real sharp end of tough reporting, out there with the boys in the minefields. The press in action.

The *Mail* raised his bottle of Pils invitingly. As all the camera team had to offer was an exhausted chocolate milk shake, I climbed out of the car. The *Mail* passed me the bottle.

'What's happening?' I asked. The public, and indeed some news editors, are under the cosy impression that reporters on a story are all out to beat the hell out of each other. Well, yes, sometimes, but only sometimes. This was not the occasion to try and be Wonderwoman.

'We've tried to go in,' said the *Mail*. 'No deal. The police are being polite but definite. There aren't any other entrances.'

I drank my Pils thoughtfully. If there's one truth every reporter knows it's that there is *always* a way in, even if it's just very slightly illegal. I went for a little walk around the block.

'You'll get jailed,' said the Cameraman.

'It's trespass,' said the Soundman.

'And don't look at us,' added the Cameraman.

I rang the News Desk.

'There are,' I said, very cautiously, and not at all sure of the reaction, 'some flats for sale in the block. Now, perhaps someone could phone up the agent and make an appointment, but not in my name which could just possibly be recognised, while I go and change my appearance slightly.'

Wild enthusiasm at the other end of the line.

'Can you check with the lawyers?' I asked.

Sure, they'd check. I might be a real tough lady hackette, but my contract with ITN didn't include spending a night in the nick for trespass. My mum wouldn't like it.

'And,' I added, 'there's just about no chance of getting

anything — even if I do get in. But it's better than hanging about on the pavement.'

An hour and a half later I was in a taxi, armed with an order to view. I had told the other reporters what I was up to, as the whole scheme would be wrecked if they tried to get in on the act.

None of us expected Blunt to answer the door; but at least it was something to do.

I descended from the taxi, swept grandly past the assembled press — who gazed speechless at this vision in a velvet suit with three inches of make-up and a swept-up hairdo — and into the block.

It was staggering. I was waved past police, past the porter who called me 'madam', and up to the flat. I resolved to spend a bit more cash on my clothes in future.

The flat for sale was fifty-eight grand for a fifty-odd-year lease. For that money, I'd have wanted something a bit more splendid. There was an insignificant bedroom, a positively miserable kitchen with no room to swing a casserole, and a bathroom with a pink suite and a fluffy pink loo cover. The living-room was long and narrow with lots of mirrors, which made it look like a little room trying to look bigger.

I think the owner smelt a rat.

'Are you buying this for yourself?'

I gave him to understand that I had a rich protector. Very rich. After a decent interval, I said I didn't think the flat was quite what I was looking for.

'A bit on the small side,' I said, with genuine disgust, and escaped into the corridor.

To my horror I found that what looked like one block at the front was actually built in an 'E' shape. Each prong of the E was totally detached from the others. The only way across was to go through the downstairs hall — at present guarded by police and porter.

I was in the central prong of the E. Blunt's flat was in the prong to my left. There was no chance of being able to walk through the hall and up to his flat. The porter would catch me. But, after all the build-up I had given to the News Desk, let alone to the antici-pating crowd outside, I couldn't just meekly give up like Rice Crispies under hot milk. . . .

I sneaked along a corridor, trying to see if there was any possible way to get across. At the end of the corridor was a fire escape from where I could see Blunt's block. I began to feel like one of those cops in American movies, preparing for the Big Effort. I could see a way to get to Blunt's front door, but I didn't like it one bit.

In the end, fear of the News Desk overcame other, more sensible terrors, and I crept on to the fire escape. My steps seemed to ring out as I tiptoed down, shaking like a leaf. Before I was halfway down, the porter walked into the courtyard, three floors below. I froze. He put something in a waste bin, then walked back inside. I carried on down.

Once in the courtyard, I crept over, bent double, to avoid being seen through any ground-floor windows, and slipped across to the fire escape at the side of Blunt's block.

I still had to get on to Blunt's floor, and shivered my way upstairs, expecting to be caught at any moment.

Blunt's flat was unmistakeable, even if I hadn't had the number. The Yale lock was reinforced by a couple of professional-looking models, and there was a spy-hole in the door. I rang the bell. Nothing. Then rang again. I didn't really expect anyone to answer, but it was worth a try. There was not a sound from the flat. I walked down the main staircase, past the astonished porter, and into the arms of my colleagues.

I was still shaking but, in the end, what was the use? It was a good effort, but useless in news terms. Still, it showed the News Desk I'd been trying to earn my pay.

We kept up the stake-out for another couple of days, but there was no sign of activity. The Pils drinkers had begun to line up their empty bottles like ninepins on top of the neat little wall bordering the flats, and this was enraging residents even more. We seemed to be attracting all the opprobrium which more properly belonged to Professor Blunt.

The last ditch effort to disturb the Professor's peace was when the *Daily Telegraph* and I tried to get through the service entrance. The *Telegraph* reporter was in his fifties, very smart in a blue wool coat and looking quite unlike a stake-out hack. A builder, working on the block, told us he knew a way in. We climbed up a service stair on to the roof where he pointed to a ladder leaning precariously against another higher roof.

'There's a skylight up there,' he said.

I could feel the colour draining from my face. I looked at the *Telegraph*. He looked at me. He shook his head.

'No, that really would be trespass. Anyway, it's too dangerous.'

We gave up. Next day ITN called off the stake-out. So did Fleet Street. But we left the little line of bottles on the wall to annoy the natives.

It was some months after these events that I was interviewing a former Home Secretary about the unconnected, if not unrelated, topic of phone tapping. The *New Statesman* had published a detailed account of the alleged phone tapping activities going on in a Post Office building near the Chelsea barracks.

The politician had agreed to be interviewed at his home. I won't say where that is, as former Home Secretaries, especially those with any connection with Northern Ireland, are regarded as being at such risk that they never go out without their pet Special Branch man.

The interview was going quite well until a gentle hum began near my left ear. I tried to swivel my eyes to see what was going on while attempting to look as if I was listening to Mr Politician. The hum became louder. I became more cross-eyed.

'Cut it,' groaned the Soundman.

'It's the mag,' said the Cameraman, proceeding to take bits off the camera.

'Terribly sorry about this,' I muttered.

The Cameraman pushed and pulled things for a few minutes, then we started again. Two minutes later the hum began again.

'Look, I'm really sorry, sir,' said I in the well-practised tones of one who's said the same thing far too many times before.

In the background more fiddling from the Cameraman. We get back to phone tapping. This time the camera doesn't just buzz, it shrieks and grinds to a protesting standstill.

So there we were, with bite-sized pieces of camera spread out on the nice living-room carpet. To add to the excitement, BBC radio were due any minute.

While the Cameraman struggled with his load of clockwork junk, the politician chatted on about phone tapping, spies and patriotism. Suddenly, apropos of nothing at all, he mentioned

Anthony Blunt. I wondered if he was rehearsing for his memoirs.

'Of course, I knew about it when I became Home Secretary,' he said. 'But it happened a long time ago.' He shook his head. 'It was all a long time ago.' And then the camera decided to work again, so he changed the subject.

Long time ago or not, it had been a story that had left a nasty taste. A really dirty job. Although it's quite usual to have to do physically nasty stories, they usually give the reporter quite a kick, especially when they're all over. But there was something mentally unpleasant about the Blunt story. Still, there are dirty jobs and dirty jobs, and at least when it's all in the mind, you don't have to get your feet wet.

And if there is one thing in life that is dead certain, it's that a News Editor with something really horrible lurking in his devious soul will look round for a nicely scented lady to drop right in it.

'I've got a good one for you tomorrow,' said the News Editor. 'Tell you after lunch.'

'Tell me now,' I pleaded, aware that, as I was being taken out to lunch by the Current Bloke, I might be a touch less suspicious than usual after half a bottle of Valpolicella.

'After lunch,' he said, and left at speed.

Lunch was smashing. We went to Bertorelli's and I had artichokes, pheasant and someone else paying for it. But I should never have had that fourth (or was it fifth?) glass of wine. By the time I got back to the Newsroom I was feeling rather mellow — also slightly guilty as it was half past three. Even so, I should have realised something was up when my chat with the News Desk began.

'It's your day off tomorrow. You don't have to do it.' His voice tailed off. 'So and so was going to do it, but she's sick.'

Well, I was full of expensive cooking and goodwill.

'Sure I'll work tomorrow. Now, what's the story?'

The News Editor inspected some papers on his desk with quite unnecessary attention.

'You know there's a chance of a water strike?'

Long pause. I suddenly realised that two or three people nearby were pretending not to listen to the conversation. The News Desk assistant was eating a sandwich with intense concentration and avoiding my eye.

114

'Well,' said the News Editor, 'we've fixed up for you to go down a sewer.' He began to talk very quickly before I recovered. 'It's quite simple. They'll fit you out with protective clothes, and there'll be breathing equipment and so on. You can go down and watch the men working, then send the film back with your recorded commentary.' He stopped and looked at me hopefully. I couldn't think of anything to say, so he carried on. 'Mind you, some of it might be tricky. They were muttering something about lowering the camera on a rope.'

I began to see why so and so had prudently gone sick. By now, everyone had given up all pretence of not listening, and the assistant was grinning over a fistful of salt beef sandwich.

'You don't *have* to do it,' said the News Editor, as a kind of afterthought.

'I suppose', I asked, clutching at straws, 'that you have found a film crew to do this?'

He nodded cheerfully.

When I took out the clippings on sewers from our library, I didn't feel any better. It seemed sewers were dark and nasty places, much infested by rats. I photocopied a few of the more gruesome ones, which gave colourful details about how everything from measles to Black Death would be unleashed if the sewage system broke down, then Julie and I went out for an early dinner.

'I doubt I'm going to feel like much breakfast,' I groaned. 'So I might as well have a last square meal.'

'They *eat* rats in parts of South America,' said Julie, dissecting her chicken.

Next morning, I slid into sewage headquarters trying to look unobtrusive.

'That bird's here now,' yelled someone.

My crew sat in a small room in attitudes of dejection, drinking tea.

'Look at that lot,' said the Lights Man. He pointed to a heap of jeans, shirts, helmets and thigh boots which smelt strongly of disinfectant.

'You don't half pick them,' said the Cameraman.

We all stood and looked at the protective clothing. A bloke from the public employees' union was going down too, both to stop us from doing anything silly, and to give an interview.

Management were keeping out of it, rather wisely I thought.

The union man was called Terry. He was a cheerful, red-cheeked individual who looked like an ad for country butter and eggs. He'd have been a sensation on *What's My Line?*. I would have sworn he was a farmworker or a seaman — something healthy and open-air. The only underground thing about him was a definitely malicious sense of humour.

'If you fall in,' he said, 'close your eyes and mouth. Don't hang on to anyone else or you'll pull them in too.'

I swallowed hard and the camera crew were beginning to look distinctly twitchy.

Terry grinned. 'Don't worry, we'll have breathing apparatus with us.'

We piled into our own cars and drove to the site of operations. It was under a large estate in North London, and to get to it we were going to have to climb through a hole in the road about two feet square. We had taken the protective gear with us in the cars. Sewage workers change on site, in large vans equipped with running water. Terry explained this was in case they got splashed, so they could wash at once. After work they would go back to headquarters, shower and change into clean clothes.

'Take all your own clothes off before you put on the protective stuff,' said Terry.

The Lights Man wanted to keep on his own trousers under the Water Board's jeans.

'Okay,' said Terry, and added in an excessively matter-of-fact tone, 'but how are you going to get home if you slip and fall in?'

The Lighting Engineer took off his trousers.

I was standing, facing modestly away from all these preparations, getting more and more unhappy. I decided to keep my underwear on and dispose of it later. This was going to be quite bad enough without having aerodynamic problems from unsupported flesh.

The sewage workers had prised up a small metal lid in the road and a narrow ladder led down to black and endless depths. There was a pervasive smell of sewage and chemicals. Terry was bouncing around being a right little ray of sunshine.

'People *will* mix different disinfectants in their lavs,' he said, his red cheeks glowing with enthusiasm. 'They don't seem to realise that when it says 'don't mix' on the pack — don't. You can get an explosion. Very nasty if you're on the lav at the time.'

The crew all giggled at this, but I was, for once, one step ahead. I gestured speechlessly down the hole.

'Yes, you get explosions down there too. If the gaffer says to get the hell out — run.' He stopped. 'Otherwise you'll get pushed over in the rush by our men.' He grinned happily.

'Just how high is it down there?' said the Lighting Man, beginning to show definite symptoms of funk.

'Not too bad — about four feet high.' There was a pause as he looked at us. The Cameraman was six foot. Terry, at about my height, a mere five and a half feet, looked up at him. 'You're going to have a bit of a problem filming,' he told us, as if we hadn't already worked that out for ourselves.

The crew climbed down the ladder first. I followed. Terry insisted that I be roped up.

'It would be dreadful publicity for the pay claim if you fell in.'

'Thanks,' I said.

Climbing down wasn't too bad. Once you got over the pitch dark and the shock of the smell, and the clammy walls on which some sort of brown fungus seemed to be growing. It was uncomfortably warm. A strand of hair fell from under my helmet, but my rubber gloves were covered with muck so I couldn't push it back.

The heat and moisture were making the camera lens fog up. So we stood in a tunnel, with the ominous noise of running water in the background, trying to dry it out.

Then down some steep slippery steps. Terry held my arm. For all his merry quips he had a sound grasp of what was good press relations.

'Don't lean on the walls,' he said suddenly. 'You get things.'

'Things?'

He didn't elaborate.

At the bottom of the steps was the sewer itself. About two feet six wide and four feet high. Men were wading along it, crouched, pushing buckets of silt they'd been dredging. This was hauled to the surface through another manhole.

Terry and I waded into the centre of the channel for an interview. I tried not to think about what was flowing round my legs.

117

Terry's cheer departed when we talked about a possible strike. The union had clearly known their stuff when they sent him to cope with us.

'We'll have sewage flowing through the streets of London. And not just London, every other city as well.'

That was all he said. It was enough.

Then it was time for a piece to camera. Well, there was no chance that I wasn't going to get my mug on the screen in a location like this. The sewer roof was so low that I had to crouch.

'Get your bottom down, Sarah,' the Cameraman kept saying. 'You look like a duck.'

I looked straight at the camera but couldn't help seeing unmentionable things swimming past, just out of the corner of my eyes. Then the crew waded along to film the sewer workers. The Cameraman had to crouch low in the fast-flowing brown river. Every so often there would be an extra rush of water as a subsidiary channel gushed into the main stream. I'd had enough. I struggled back up the steps. When the fresh air hit, it made me so dizzy I had to be pulled on to the pavement. I sat, collapsed, in the road. The crew fell out a few minutes later. The first thing they did was light cigarettes.

'Go away,' I said, 'I've given them up.' If I could survive this without a cigarette, I'd survive anything.

We all sat in the street gasping. Terry climbed out — the picture of exuberant health.

'That wasn't so bad, was it? How was my interview?'

'Just great,' I said and relapsed into silence.

Terry looked at us. 'You want to take all that gear off, then go straight home and shower.'

We weren't going to argue.

Back home I used two full bottles of Dettol in the shower and chucked out all the underwear I had kept on. I showered for half an hour and washed my hair, then had a bath and washed my hair again, then another shower, then went back to the office, drenched in Arpège.

The story was smashing, loaded with nice, crunchy words like 'typhoid' and 'cholera'. Even the Deputy Editor emerged from his office to congratulate, though I noticed he stayed at a safe distance.

For several days our colleagues gave the crew and me an ostentatiously wide berth. One advantage: it cleared a quick route to the tea trolley.

I kept having to fight the urge to scratch. Still, I got my own back. When I put in my expenses, one item read:

'To: ladies bra — four pounds.'

'What', said my boss, 'did you do with your bra?'

'Burnt it, of course. What else?'

He looked at me, wondering whether this was just a fresh line in fiddles. I started to undo my blouse, very slowly.

'Shall I show you?'

He took my word for it.

'Just don't ask me why I earn my money,' I said to Julie on the phone next day. 'I'm tired out, had to chuck out half my underwear, and I keep getting an overwhelming passion to have another bath. 'What's more,' I continued in grieved tones, the local kids have tried to break into my flat again.' Julie made soothing noises.

'Did they take anything?'

'No, the woman upstairs chased them.' I sneezed. 'Did you see my sewers story? The Editor sent me a note saying it was good.'

'No,' she said. 'I was out.'

'My storage heaters have broken down again,' I moaned, then I registered what she'd said. 'Out with who?' I asked suspiciously.

'I don't think I've mentioned him before,' she sighed, in a breathy sort of voice. 'Anyway, don't you mean "with whom"?'

'I know,' I said. 'Can you hang on to my dress?'

'How did you guess?' she murmured. 'You are sweet.'

'Grrh,' I said.

I hung up and went to kick the cold radiators. Then I settled down to an intense study of estate agents' lists. There's a certain poetic prose about estate agents' descriptions that ensure many a wasted visit to view some quite impossible hovels. Finally I found one that sounded exactly what I was looking for: 'Large living-room with elegant cornice; modern polished wood stairs to enormous bedroom, modern bath off. Full gas central heating, two minutes from Hampstead Heath.' The price was a bit high for one bedroom but it seemed worth a visit.

The street was quiet enough and tree-lined, but as far as I could work out the only way to get to the Heath in two minutes would be by helicopter. A railway line had somehow managed to get in the way. The living-room was about ten feet square, with an embarrassed looking bit of fibreglass masquerading as a cornice, and a lump of tatty plaster hanging on to the ceiling trying to look like a centre Victorian rose.

The builders had apparently forgotten about a kitchen, but there was an electric cooker point tucked coyly on the wall beside the front door. The modern staircase took up a good quarter of the floor space.

'Nice and elegant, isn't it?' said the estate agent's rep. 'Just right for a fashionable young bachelor girl like yourself.'

'The word you are looking for is "spinster",' I said in what I hoped were appropriately vinegary tones.

'Why don't you look upstairs?' he said. 'Lovely big double bedroom.'

I was tempted not to bother, but climbed wearily up the stairs, looked round and then negotiated my way down with difficulty.

'Those stairs are killers,' I remarked as I skidded back to ground level. 'Anyway, it's not what I'm looking for. I want two bedrooms and a proper fitted kitchen. And I don't want the loo leading out of my bedroom.'

'You won't get that at the price you're prepared to pay,' he said wisely.

I stomped out and retrieved my minicab which was waiting patiently. This was the sixth flat I'd seen that day.

'No?' The helpful driver had been following my progress with interest. This was the fifth day he'd taken me out flat hunting. I'd given myself a fortnight to find something that would suit both me and the Woolwich and was beginning to despair.

'Home,' I said, putting my head in my hands.

'Miss Cullen,' he said, 'I don't know what you're looking for, but I passed a big block in Highgate that had For Sale signs up. It looked quite smart.'

'I can't afford to live in Highgate. Highgate is where people who find Hampstead too vulgar hang out. And priced accordingly.' But we went up to Highgate anyway to take a look.

'It's a very big block,' I said. It was one of those vast thirties-style buildings, where you expect to see signs to the Captain's office. If you put a couple of funnels on top it could call itself the Queen Mary and sail down the Thames.

There was a porter on the door. I decided this was definitely out of my price bracket. 'Any flats for sale?' We descended to the lower depths of the building.

'An artistic basement,' said the porter, with a jolly little laugh.

But the flat was on garden level, and had two nice white bedrooms, a neat little fitted kitchen, a reasonable living-room and a modern tiled bathroom.

'Isn't it clean!' I sighed, rather giving away my bargaining position. I took another look round.

'How much?'

It was just slightly less than I had been prepared to pay. I phoned the agent and offered two hundred less. They accepted.

Outside I sank into the cab in stunned silence. The driver looked sympathetic. 'No good?'

'No, yes, it's great, thanks for the suggestion,' I said. 'It's perfect.'

'Back home?'

'No, Holborn. I want to talk to my building society.'

'And the best thing of all,' I breathed ecstatically, 'is that it's got lovely, lovely central heating.'

SARAH CULLEN...
...NEWS AT TEN...
..GLUB.. GLUB...

# 8

## HARD WORK

It took just four weeks from seeing the flat to moving in. The building society produced the cash amiably enough and my solicitor broke all records doing the conveyancing. I reckoned I was due some rent back on my old flat, but my former landlord, who had been indicating for months that he'd like me to move as he wanted to sell up, now did a quick reverse.

'I'm entitled to a month's notice,' said he, 'so I'll keep the rent instead.'

'But you wanted me to move,' I wailed. 'You've been going on about selling the house for months.

'What's more,' he said, going into attack, 'you can't have all your deposit back, you've broken lightbulbs. Lightbulbs are very expensive these days.'

I took the tube up to Highgate to have a fresh look at my new home and cheer myself up. The porter met me, carrying a wet rag and wearing an expression of gratified gloom.

'You left the tap on last time you were here. I saw the water coming out from under the door.'

I ˜quelched into the bathroom, the porter in my wake. The tap was wearing an innocent look and dripping gently.

'Needs a new washer,' said the porter redundantly.

A drowned cockroach reposed in the wash basin.

'Do you get many of those round here?' I indicated it in a carefully offhand fashion.

'Only when we're cleaning the boilers,' he said. We locked the door. 'You'll need a new lock on that,' said the porter. 'We've had a lot of break-ins lately.'

As I left a woman came up to him. 'Why is the hot water off again?' A long explanation involving boilers and descaling pursued me into the street.

The flat had time to dry out, because for the next few weeks I hardly had a chance to get back there. The firemen were on strike and the News Desk had set up a unit called, pessimistically, 'Fire Watch'. Reporters and crews working on the story took it in turns to stay overnight in a central London hotel. If there was a serious fire we'd be alerted and have to tumble out and get on the story. With their infallible flair for discomfort the desk booked us into a grimly modern establishment near Euston. They stopped serving food — any food, even sandwiches — at eleven in the evening, which meant we had just time to get back after *News at Ten* and see the restaurant shutting up shop for the night. The first night I arrived they didn't have a room for me and one was only produced after forty-five minutes of hanging round the lobby.

'Do you think I could have some coffee?'

'Coffee? But it's half past eleven at night!' This from a porter who looked suspiciously as if he were wearing mascara.

The firemen's strike had the indefinable glamour that industrial action rarely acquires. The combination of firemen standing outside their stations, a brazier of charcoal blazing away, and the army struggling to fill the gap, whizzing round in ancient fire engines known as 'Green Goddesses' clanging the bell by hand, had a kind of irrestible lunacy about it.

The firemen had considerable talent for good public relations and by a stroke of sheer genius asked people who supported their case to hoot their car horns as they drove past each picket line. Especially in the first days of the strike the air was filled with tootling horns.

However, the army aren't slow off the mark either when it comes to good publicity, so images of gallant and underpaid firemen were nicely balanced by pictures of clean-limbed youths struggling with fire hoses and striking attitudes reminiscent of photos of the Blitz. 'Struggling' was frequently the operative word; at some of the fires I went to it wasn't clear whether one was in most danger of being boiled or drowned by over-enthusiastic hose work.

The problem with being on this sort of standby is that you either toss and turn all night waiting for the phone to ring, or you decide to be practical and take a sleeping pill. With deathly logic it's always the night you finally capitulate to sleep that the phone rings.

'Uh huh?' I was all tangled up in blankets.

'Are you awake?' asked the News Editor.

'Uh,' I said.

'I'll phone you back in five minutes,' said the News Editor. Some News Editors are like that. Considerate. It's like seeing King Kong trying to smile. Sort of unnerving.

I fell out of bed and, after a quick attack with cold water and face flannel, was moderately alive when the phone rang again.

'Are you awake?'

'I'm dressed,' I said in an injured tone, struggling with the zip of my jeans.

'Okay,' said the News Desk and proceeded to tell me of a major fire in East London. I took down notes of the details with one hand, trying to zip myself up decently with the other. Finally I resorted to safety pins.

The crew stumbled into the hotel's reception area as I crawled out of the lift. We blinked at each other.

'Gosh, I've never seen you without make-up before,' said the Lights Man ingenuously. We tottered out to the cars, parked for the night on double yellow lines.

The factory fire in East London could very easily have turned into a major disaster. We saw it miles away, a blazing rage in the sky. But somehow fires never quite take off for me. This may be because I nearly burnt down my parents' home at five years old. My father was later heard saying that, if I'd been given a doll at Christmas instead of a junior chemistry set, they'd never have had that problem. Anyway, fires tend to recall an image of charred wallpaper and Dad sprinting round with buckets of water.

There was no question that the factory fire made excellent TV film. We arrived to see Green Goddesses drawn up and troops unravelling coils of hose. The ground was inches deep in water.

The duty officer, a youthful forty-year-old, came over to us. 'We must warn you that you are taking a risk filming here.' We all nodded in what we hoped was an encouraging fashion. 'There are nearly three hundred thousand gallons of inflammable white spirit here. It would only take a spark and they'd go off like a bomb.'

'Ulp,' I said.

'And just over there is a paint store. That would go like a rocket if the fire spreads.'

'What is actually our fire?' I asked.

'It's a warehouse, packed with waste rags.'

The army didn't seem too keen at first to let us film but after a little light banter the officer finally waved us over to somewhere we could park. We disembarked, shivering.

'I don't know why it should be so cold,' said the Cameraman, 'with all that going on.'

We shuffled across to the scene of the action. Once we'd been okayed by the officer on the gate, no one seemed to worry too much where we went or what we filmed. In that, it was very different from a police-controlled operation where you are herded away from any trouble. The army showed a refreshing reliance on our common sense.

'I think', I said to the Cameraman, 'that we ought to film those.'

Hundreds of cans of white spirit were stacked alongside the blazing warehouse. Troops were hosing them down in an attempt to keep them cool.

'Well, you'll have to go first,' said the Cameraman. This wasn't out of concern that the white spirit might go in flames. Oh no. Just ahead was an indentation in the road. All the water sloshing round had filled that up. We couldn't get to film the cans without going through it. I paddled through, water up to my knees, turned at the other side.

'Well?'

The crew followed.

'I wouldn't hang round here if I were you,' said an anonymous shape tottering under a fire hose.

'We aren't going to,' said the Cameraman with a note of finality.

Just ahead of us the *Evening Standard* photographer was on his knees in a puddle of water, lost to all else as he photographed the blaze.

'He's a nut,' the anonymous squaddie with the hose confided. At that the nut turned round to grin, 'Hi, Sarah', and returned to taking his pictures, his sharp face tight with concentration, illuminated by the flames.

'Sorry,' said the anonymity. 'Didn't know he was a friend of yours.'

The weather was on the troops' side, and ours, come to that. A strong wind blew the flames away from the chemicals, to my undisguised relief.

'Let's get a cup of tea,' said the *Evening Standard* in my ear.

'Tea?' It seemed an unlikely prospect. Indeed, he looked a touch unlikely himself; bundled up in a black leather coat, very wet, and topped off with an unshaven rakish face.

'You look,' I muttered, 'like an escapee from the Gestapo.'

'Tea,' he said firmly. 'Over there. The WVS. Such lovely ladies.'

He led me by the elbow to the little wagon dispensing tea and buns to the troops.

'Hello, my lovelies,' said he. 'How about a little tea for my frozen friend from ITN, then?' The ladies all smiled. I clutched the mug in numbed fingers and drank thankfully.

126

'I'd rather have a Guinness,' he continued under his breath, then nodded and smiled over his teacup to the WVS top lady.

'Stop complaining,' I said. 'I think they're wonderful.'

The crew had by now all found the tea wagon so we stood round wetly and discussed our next move. The flames were well under control so the obvious step was to do a 'next morning' sequence. I trotted off to check with the senior officer that we were okay to knock off for a couple of hours and go back to our horrible hotel.

My jeans were soaked thigh deep in water, but overtures to the night porter about having them dried out met with a blank stare from the mascara-fringed eyes.

'This isn't a camping site, you know,' he said chillingly. I dripped off in the direction of my bedroom leaving a little trail of puddles behind. Once towelled down, my mind turned to thoughts of brekkies.

'Do you think,' I said to the phone, 'I could have some tea and toast. Even . . .' — visions of grandeur — 'a bacon sandwich?'

'But it's six o'clock,' said the porter. 'We don't do breakfasts till seven-thirty. We don't do them before that.'

At quarter to eight, still brekkieless, we were all dressed and assembled to go and film the aftermath of last night's fire.

'I want my breakfast,' wailed a voice. We headed off in the general direction of the East End, and then detoured into a nice warm transport café for platters of bacon, eggs and beans. The only blot on this happy prospect was my jeans clinging damply to my legs.

'Looks wet, your friend,' said the waitress as she delivered our fry-up. I grinned blissfully over a tummyful of bacon and beans.

When we got back to the site of the fire we found that one factory had been totally gutted, and four nearby damaged. There was just a heap of wet rubble, still faintly smoking. The owners had arrived and drifted round, looking worried as they tried to estimate their loss. Troops were still standing by in case it flared again.

We phoned into the office and, with one of those unpleasant parallels in the news business, we were re-routed to yet another fire nearby. It was a relatively small house in Leyton but one woman had been killed and another four people injured. It was the sort of accident that could happen to any of us at any time.

While all the media had been at the factory fire, in this small terrace a woman had died. The first death in a fire in London since the strike began.

'Ironic,' said the Cameraman.

'The BBC don't use "ironic",' I said. 'Their style book bans it.'

We both looked at the blackened little house.

'It's still ironic,' he said.

The blaze seemed to have begun in a back room, probably caused by an electric fire. The house was burnt out; when we arrived it was no more than a shell. The police weren't even allowing press inside in case the whole building collapsed. Although a family living upstairs managed to escape, clambering through windows, a fifty-year-old woman on the ground floor died. The fire had been fast and vicious. Two pickets from a nearby fire station had turned up just before the troops to try and help. Even with breathing equipment they were beaten back by the flames. Three police and an RAF firefighter ended up in hospital, overcome by smoke.

By the afternoon the house was boarded up and blank, giving no idea of all the excitement and panic earlier that day.

A certain amount of concern was now beginning to develop over whether the army were suitably kitted out for the venture. The soldiers were beetling off to their various fire-fighting engagements dressed mainly in their usual army gear, including the traditional soup-plate helmets.

'Well,' said one safety expert to me, 'they do look great, and will remind all the mums of those fire-fighting days of the Blitz. Only problem is, they're not designed to cope with a modern fire.'

I was interviewing him in, of all places, ITN's underground car park. We quite often interview people in the board room but that day this was unexceptionally occupied with a board meeting. For some reason we don't have an interview room. We stopped the interview briefly as a camera car whipped off to some exciting location like the Middle East, or, more possibly, East Cheam.

The safety expert continued. 'Any modern building is a kind of heap of electrical cables and plastic building materials all wrapped round each other. And that army helmet . . .' He held up a specimen and looked at it derisively. 'Well, falling plastics can drip on to the back of a soldier's neck. It's totally unprotected.' He stopped and revolved the helmet slowly. 'And an electric cable,' said he gloatingly. 'Well, if an electric cable fell on to the helmet it would just fry the soldier up, wouldn't it?'

I phoned the firemen's union to ask if they'd be prepared to let the troops use their safety helmets. They were less than keen.

'A helmet is a very personal bit of gear, isn't it, love?'

Well, the troops might have been saying they were quite happy with their helmets, but they were showing a definite touch of irritation about the quarters they were shacked up in whilst saving London from the second Great Fire. We arrived to film what was described as a 'typical barracks', meeting the *Evening Standard* on his way out.

'Evening, darlin',' he said, flitting off into the twilight, black leather coat flapping in a bat-like fashion. 'When are you going to come and drink a pint of Guinness with me?'

'Oh, well,' I said, resigned, 'if he's here it probably means it's a moderately good story.' Then I looked at my watch. 'Anyway, he's missed his last edition, so he's had it.'

It is one of the unvarying unfairnesses of the trade that the bloke with the latest deadline is the one who gets the story. The *Evening Standard* must have been planning to do a spread for the next day, so the sight of someone with a ten o'clock deadline was like a faint drift of strychnine in the air. But the 'firewatch unit' was being co-ordinated by the Original Ace News Editor and we were enjoying being one bite ahead.

The troops called it the 'Cockroach Hilton'. For thirty-five men of the Royal Greenjackets one room had been home for a week. It was just a prefab hut behind a Territorial Army headquarters. There weren't any beds; the men were sleeping on camp mattresses on the floor.

The troops were on full alert and changed shifts every four hours, so slept in their clothes. Even if they wanted to strip, there were only occasional nails stuck in the wall on which to hang their gear. Overcoats hung unhappily from a picture hook. We filmed all this squalor enthusiastically, then asked to see the lavatories and wash rooms. These turned out to be about fifty yards from the hut, so two miserable soldiers were turfed out of their well-earned rest for our benefit and sent scurrying across the yard clutching their spongebags.

I was most surprised when we went to chat to the soldiers. I had anticipated high-level opposition to this suggestion but it was astonishingly relaxed. The Captain with us, who didn't look a day over twenty-five, pinched a bit of cake from a soldier's supper tray.

'Look at that,' said the man witheringly. 'Just look at that, stealing our food now, are they?'

Everyone roared with laughter. I'd expected it to be all 'Jump to attention' like the old films, and was amazed at the gentle abuse the officers took, not to mention the cracks flying the other way.

We set up to film the soldiers talking to me informally. Far from the presence of the Captain putting anyone off, he positively inspired a flow of protest about the living accommodation. Although they were supposed to be talking to me, every so often they'd look over at the Captain to make sure he was taking it all on board. Afterwards we toddled off to have a look at the catering arrangements. One of the big complaints had been that the ranks weren't allowed to drink alcohol on this job.

'If I left a bit for a round, would they get it?' I asked, proffering fifteen quid.

'When they get back to barracks,' said their boss, smiling. So I handed over the money.

The cookhouse was something else. Few back gardens in that respectable suburb of Bromley can ever have seen such campfire activities. When I came to record my commentary I originally described it as a 'cook-up' but was dissuaded by the Sound Engineer for linguistic reasons.

Two army cooks stood over what looked to me like two shallow pits, ablaze. On top of these perched a batch of shallow metal cans shaded by a canvas awning. It was like a marvellous, dream-like scouts expedition. From the look of it I expected some sort of horrible stew, or typical 'boys'' food, like burnt sausages. But the cooks produced a two-course supper, including a choice of roast pork with crackling and apple sauce, liver and cottage pie. The Captain, who was as thin as a rake, pinched a bit of liver on the way through. 'I always seem to do all my eating on the move,' he complained.

'I can't think why,' said I, my own mouth full of purloined apple crumble with caramel topping. 'I just wish you'd lend these two to our canteen for a week.' Adding as an afterthought, 'I couldn't cook like that even with a microwave.'

'You haven't had army training,' said the Captain.

Why is it that strikes always seem to happen in the winter, when the snow is crisping along the ground and the only place for any sensible mammal is hibernating safely in its bed? There's nothing Christmas-card-like about standing in a blinding shower of snow, trying to exchange political chat with some poor so-and-so on a picket line. Both of you are numb with cold and fatigue, but at least I'm paid for it while the men hunched over their braziers are wondering where next week's rent is coming from.

You can get rather fed up with various trade unionists who have an unpleasant tendency to patronise women reporters. The attitude is that woman journalists are 'daddy's girls'. It doesn't seem to occur to some people that we might actually have a living to earn. This occasionally manifests itself in very concrete terms.

One particular picket line was distinctly unfriendly. 'Shove off,' said a large gentleman. 'We don't want little girls round here.'

Advancing a pace he waved in a threatening manner. He can't have been very much bigger than a baby elephant.

'Don't you talk to Miss Cullen like that,' said the Sound Recordist, a freelance, abandoning his task of recording this entertaining little exchange, and moving forward protectively.

This was just about all I needed. I hauled the Recordist off into the car, where we were joined by the Cameraman, who wore a misanthropic expression.

'Did we get the sound on that last bit?' I asked. No, we hadn't because of the Sound Recordist's defence of my person. 'Why?' I wailed. 'It's not your job to do the chivalry bit.'

'Well,' said he, quite taken aback at my ungracious reaction, 'if anyone spoke to my wife like that, I wouldn't allow it.'

'I'm not your bloody wife,' I said, feeling like a blue touch paper that's just been lit. 'Next time do me a favour and keep recording.'

'Well, I don't like seeing a woman spoken to like that.'

131

'I'm not a woman,' I yelped, 'I'm a reporter.'

'I think,' said the Cameraman in a diplomatic move, 'we all might be better off for a nice cup of tea.'

I went home to find the new flat chilly despite the central heating. The whole of London seemed frozen solid, aided by yet another industrial dispute which meant the roads weren't being gritted. Light entertainment of the week was to stand by the bus stop on Highgate Hill and watch as unwary drivers tried to apply their brakes at the zebra crossing. Slithering up the hill to shop was positively menacing, while sliding down again, ballasted with the week's supply of Birds Eye, was suicidal.

On the mat, nicely timed to brighten this euphoric horizon, was a postcard from Julie. She was in the Seychelles, and I reflected, still with my dress. I hoped the dress enjoyed the holiday.

My own first experience of being on what might be called the chilly end of an industrial dispute came while I was still in training as a writer. I'd hardly got my foot past the front door before we were all sitting on the steps trying to look like a picket line.

The dispute was over pay — very important to us at the time but historically of no great note; everyone seemed to be going on strike over pay at that precise moment. Union meetings were held in an upstairs room at the local pub, the Green Man, and packed to the door.

I frankly couldn't follow much of the argument as I'd hardly been in the job a year, and still found it surprising that anyone was prepared to pay me for such enjoyable work. This, I might add, is a sentiment you grow out of, at about the same time as you acquire an inflationary mortgage.

The chapel voted to go out; so out we went. We all had to sign a roster saying when we'd be on picket duty; really it was exactly like being at work but without the loot. I had one memorable evening on the last picket line shift, ten till eleven at night.

A Senior Correspondent was on duty, and he had in his pocket a flask of malt whisky. I was all of twenty-two and whatever vices I had, or indeed have, a taste for whisky isn't one of them. Wine, yes, but whisky I find unpleasant. However, it was freezing cold, and I was shivering in my socks.

'Try this,' said the Kindly Correspondent, beaming avuncularly.

'Nice,' I said. It went down like water. It was obviously the best stuff. I don't know if you've ever had whisky in the open air on a freezing cold night, when you have literally never tasted the stuff except with hot water and lemon as a cold cure? Well, it's great.

I was fine while we were outside, but once the picket duty was over and we went to the pub, the union HQ for the duration, the warm air inside finished me off and I got very giggly.

The Kindly Correspondent was looking at me in considerable alarm. I wasn't tight enough not to see that. He clearly felt he was responsible for this horribly happy female. When I said that I hadn't had scotch before, except when I'd had a cold, he looked distinctly miserable. In all my time as an adult, I have never been so firmly told it was time to go home. The poor man marched me out to his car and dumped me unceremoniously at my front door, hanging painfully by the kerb to see if I'd manage to negotiate my keys.

It wasn't till the next day, through an agonising headache, that I realised how lucky I was he'd seen me home, and not left me to the tender mercies of my more youthful colleagues. The indiscretions of members of the media have a nasty habit of turning into highly entertaining reading in *Private Eye*. Great fun, unless you're the idiot who's been indiscreet. . . .

# 9

## GOSSIP

When I first became a journalist I assumed that my function would be to find out how other people got on with their lives. It never for one moment crossed my mind that my own activities — that daily round of picket lines, hospitals, fires, and pandas — might be a subject for speculation. But the 'Dog Eat Dog' mentality has evolved into one of 'Dog Watches Dog'.

You can always tell when the news is getting a bit thin — when the newspapers are filled with interviews by one journalist of another journalist about what it's like to be a journalist. TV has added a new dimension to this. The newscasters, especially the ladies, are automatically superstars, and a flash of thigh is a front-page headline. But even we lesser fry benefit from the stardust they sprinkle. Our routine of picket line, hospital and stake-out can be made to sound very glamorous. I've been interviewed on the odd occasion for magazines, and quite enjoyed it.

But there's another side to all this wonderful publicity — and that's when something goes wrong. And the worst day I had really was nothing to do with me at all.

I'd been out for lunch with my Aunt Mildred. Now, as Mildred is seventy-five, a retired history lecturer, and a stalwart of the University Women's Club, that might not sound a particularly hazardous undertaking. I met her at the club, a distinguished and low-key establishment in South Audley Street. It's very soft and quiet, with donnish old ladies reading the *Telegraph* over their sherry, and donnish younger ones doing exactly the same. Mildred had taken me to lunch there once — the day of the school dinner is not dead — but since she had retired, she had suddenly blossomed forth and shown a previously unexpected appreciation of a good meal in sybaritic surroundings.

Mildred wanted to discuss a projected trip to China, as she was concerned she might be just a wee bit too old. She was just back from a month long tour of the States, and was planning a quick reviving break in the Middle East as a kind of chaser. So I spent lunch reassuring her that, in her case, age had nothing to do with it.

Over the armagnac we left the subject of travel and she grilled me on my love life. I told her it was very staid. She didn't altogether believe me.

Auntie wandered off cheerfully to look for a camping shop to buy a good anti-mosquito device, and I headed back to the office. I had been working on a story that morning, hoping to film it later in the week, and I needed to get hold of my immediate boss to approve some details. He wasn't in the Newsroom, and as it was not quite three o'clock, I betook myself to the local hostelry to see if he was there.

I was feeling especially elegant that day, as I had just bought a new pair of shoes from a rather smart establishment. They'd been in a sale at thirteen pounds reduced from twenty-six, blue with very high, chic heels. I teetered into the pub and had a chat with the boss, virtuously refusing all offers of a drink. Then I teetered out again to get on with the job.

There's a small step leading out of the pub on to the pavement. It can't be more than two inches high. The nice new shoes obviously thought I'd been keeping low company, because the next thing I knew I was sitting on the pavement, the heel of one shoe twisted right over, and my ankle swelling rapidly and starting to go an unusual colour.

'Can I help?' a stray gentleman rushed up. Nice man.

'I've got some friends inside.' I'd noticed the Industrial Correspondent just by the door. 'Perhaps you wouldn't mind asking them . . .'

'Not at all.' He shot back into the pub.

When the Industrial Correspondent came out, he roared with laughter. I was in quite some pain, and didn't see the funny side at all.

The Stray Man looked at him in surprise, and said, 'Well, I'll help you, dear.'

I don't at all mind being called 'dear' in this sort of circumstance, and gave him a dazzling smile. At that, company loyalty reasserted itself, and some of my colleagues who had gathered to watch the fun helped me back to the office.

By now it was obvious the ankle was sprained, if not worse. So after half an hour moaning gently in a corner of the Newsroom, I enlisted one of my friends as support and hopped round the corner to the Middlesex Hospital. The staff there also thought it was a great laugh when I explained I'd been coming out of the pub. I was getting used to this reaction. They X-rayed me, decided it was just a sprain, and gave me a very impressive bandage. They also produced some pain-relieving tablets and I began to feel pleasurably light-headed.

There was still the small matter of the shoe. I booked a mini-cab to take me home, then changed my mind.

'Let's go to Oxford Street. I want to take the shoe back.'

'Are you sure that's wise?' The driver glanced at me, eyebrows raised. 'You don't look very well.' This was true; I was barefoot, bandaged, and my face streaked with Lancôme brown-black mascara.

'None of this would have happened but for the shoe,' I said.

We went to complain. After the rehearsal with the heater I was viciously confident.

I padded barefoot across the gritty pavement and into the shop. The carpet was nice and thick to my bare tootsies. I dangled the offending shoes in one hand and within seconds an assistant shot up and asked me what I wanted. I displayed the shoe. The assistant was Spanish, and her English wasn't very good, but she didn't agree that she should change the shoes, although the heel was literally bent in two.

'We don't change, it's not our fault,' she kept saying in phrase-book English. I had done more than enough stories on consumer legislation and consumer rights to know that I was entitled to my money back. It was the first day I had worn the shoes, and they had been used only for very normal purposes; I mean, I might have had to climb over a wall in them, or even run down a street. But I hadn't.

'I suppose you are allowed to walk in them?' I asked sarcastically. This was wasted; she just repeated, 'Not our fault. Nothing wrong with shoes.'

A number of other customers were looking with fascination at me and the shoes. In the end I summoned the manageress, one of those rigid ladies with impossibly well-pressed skirts and matching well-ironed faces, lacquered with cosmetics.

She was English, but her logic wasn't any better.

'We've never had any complaints about these shoes before. There's been no trouble with the heel. Anyway you bought them in the sale.' She stared at me in a manner designed to reduce me to apology.

Now, the law of the land says that goods bought in a sale must be capable of doing what they're supposed to do, unless the customer is specifically told that they're broken. In other words, if you buy a radio in a sale and it doesn't work, you can get your money back. Similarly shoes are made for walking in, and

137

this pair caved in on their first outing.

I recited all this to the manageress. When I stopped for breath, she said, 'There's never been any complaint before. I think you bent the heel deliberately.' I gave her a quick run down on the law of slander, then announced that the shop would be hearing from my solicitor. This was rather overdoing things, but a solicitor's letter doesn't cost much and even the threat can have a startling effect.

It worked. Indeed, it worked so well that, instead of giving me simply a replacement pair of sales goods, I was presented with a pair of sandals costing forty-eight pounds. Forty-eight pounds — I don't know anyone who'd pay that sort of money for *sandals*. I've still got them, and very nice they are too.

I thanked the manageress sweetly, remembering the Churchillian dictum: 'If you have to shoot a man, it costs nothing to be polite', and limped back out to the minicab, where I gleefully displayed my trophy to the driver.

'Well, I'm glad you're satisfied,' he said, 'because it's cost you three pounds in waiting time for this cab.'

Who was it who said that every silver lining has a cloud wrapped round it?

My ankle was still hurting despite the combined effect of the lunch and the pills, so I was glad to get home and limp to the flat. The porter gave me an arm to the front door. I staggered through, and flaked out on my bed.

I must have been deeply asleep, when I heard someone hammering on the door. I burrowed down under the duvet. I wasn't expecting visitors, and anyone who had turned up without being invited could just take themselves off again. The hammering continued, then I heard Julie's voice; she was back from the Seychelles.

'Sarah, wake up. It's me, Julie.'

I staggered to the door and let her in. She stared at my unwashed face.

'You look dreadful.'

'I *feel* dreadful.' We went into the living-room, where I caved in all over the settee.

'I've been knocking on your door for ages. You answered once about ten minutes ago but must have gone straight off to sleep again.' I nodded; I was feeling very dopey.

'Look,' said Julie, 'you've got to pull yourself together. There's real trouble.' I stared blankly. 'The *Sunday Shock and Horror* are waiting outside with a camera. They won't tell me what they want.'

'What!' I yelled, in sheer surprise. 'I haven't done anything, have I?' in the tones of one expecting to be blamed for something.

While I had been blissfully unconscious, quite a little drama had been going on in the front hall. A woman from one of the less refined Sunday papers had turned up, plus a photographer, and walked into the flats. Heaven knows where they had got my address from. Luckily for me the porter was on duty, and waylaid them.

'What do you want?'

'Sarah Cullen's expecting us,' they said cheekily.

'Oh, she is, is she?' He was suspicious because of my sprained ankle. If I'd been expecting visitors, he thought I'd probably have mentioned it.

'Well,' he said, 'she's not very well. I think I'd better ask if she expects you.'

It was at this point, dead on cue, that Julie arrived. She had rung my office and been told I'd gone home with a sprained ankle, so decided to come round and see how things were going. The porter recognised her.

'This is a friend of Miss Cullen's. Perhaps you had better speak to her.'

Well, the reporter might, mistakenly, have thought she could fool the porter, but after one look at Julie, she decided she had met her match. Julie's fragile, blonde looks might confuse blokes, but not women.

'What do you want?' asked Julie.

The paper declined to explain why they wanted to talk to me, so Julie refused even to ask if I would see them. The porter took her aside.

'Miss Cullen really isn't at all well,' he said. 'Otherwise I'd just have let them go down, and tipped her off through the house

139

phone. But she's hurt her leg and she's a bit, well, shall we say over-relaxed.'

Julie went back to the reporter.

'It's out of the question. Anyway, if you want to see Sarah you should phone her office.' Then the porter firmly showed them out the front door.

After I'd heard this story, I began to come round — from shock as much as anything. 'What are they doing now?' I asked, with a curious sense of the tables being turned.

'Standing behind a tree on the lawn glaring at the porter. He's standing at the front door glaring back. I think he's quite enjoying himself.'

The head porter is a man of military bearing who doesn't wear a uniform on duty, but sportsjacket and flannels. He is extremely imposing. He'd be dining out on this story for weeks.

'Well, what do they want?' asked Julie.

'I've no idea.' I was wholly baffled.

'I'll make you some coffee, you're going to need it,' said Julie.

There was a knock on the door. I bolted to the lavatory and locked it. If necessary, I could climb out the window, sprained ankle and all. False alarm, it was the porter. He came in and had some coffee. He had locked the front door, so only residents with keys could get in. I explained that I had no idea what it was all about.

'Shall I call the police if they don't go?' he asked, cracking his knuckles in an anticipatory fashion.

Well, it was very tempting, but I thought that was going a bit far. Besides, I had disturbed a few people's peace myself on occasion.

'No, they're only doing their job.'

The porter looked as if he thought I was mad. Next the phone rang. It was the reporter. I still couldn't work out how they had found either my address or phone number.

'Is that Sarah Cullen?'

'Who is that?'

'This is So and So from the *Sunday Shock and Horror*. Can you tell me about your relationship with So-and-So?'

'Who?'

'We understand you go out with him.'

'What?'

I was genuinely surprised. This was the first time I had heard about it.

So and So was a *nauseatingly* rich young man who occasionally made the gossip columns.

'I think', said I, 'that someone has been spinning you a line. You're chasing an extremely elusive wild goose.'

'Well, we've been told you go out with him,' she continued, nothing daunted. I was so relieved by this stage that I laughed. I had been expecting all sorts of disaster and instead it was just this bit of nonsense.

'I'm really sorry to tell you this, but you really have made a mistake.'

I was being very polite because of my own experience. If someone loses their temper with me I assume they have something to hide. The upshot was that she clearly believed me, apologised for disturbing me, and said goodbye.

That was the end of the matter, except when I retailed the episode next day at a dinner party nobody seemed to think it was at all funny.

'Someone you know,' said a friend, 'must have leaked them that story. Some people have a very strange sense of humour. Think how embarrassing it might have been.'

In fact I was thinking about my Current Bloke. He was 'something in the City' and rather given to formal public manners plus Savile Row suits.

None of this had prepared me for my experiences the first time I went to his flat. I was carefully applying more lipstick, and reached out for some loo paper to blot it with. The loo roll suddenly moved. Then it took off at high speed round the bathroom. Its speed had nothing on mine as I leaped on top of the loo and started having a most indecorous screaming fit.

'What is it?' a concerned voice inquired from the other side of the locked door.

I continued to scream, even more loudly as I'd just spotted a small pink nose with whiskers protruding from one end of the roll. The bathroom was by now being draped with pink Andrex,

141

as the loo roll continued to rush round.

'What *is* it?' said the voice in some alarm.

'Aaaaa, there's something . . .'

'It's a hamster.' Pause. 'A hamster. It's my brother's. I'm looking after it while he's on holiday.' Pause. 'Are you all right?'

I opened the door. 'Do you mean to tell me that you let me just walk in there? Didn't you think I might be a bit surprised?'

'Watch out,' he interrupted. 'It's escaping.' The loo roll pelted past. Four very small feet were just visible. It vanished under a bookcase. It took us half an hour to tempt it out with bits of apple.

'This was supposed to be a romantic evening,' said Bloke as he took me home. I remained wrapped in frozen silence. 'Can I see you again?'

I cracked. 'I don't see why not. Anyway, I've got just the thing.'

'Mmm?'

'A couple of complimentary tickets.'

'What for?'

'The Zoo!'

Gossip, of course, is one of the problems of working in TV. Things do happen that would make a good line in the gossip columns, but generally people don't split on their colleagues. Occasionally, however, human nature being what it is, they do. Sometimes the result is just amusing. Once a newscaster broke a tooth midway through the morning and had to rush off to a dentist. This duly turned up in a gossip column the next day. On another occasion a Labour MP arrived for an interview without a jacket and borrowed the producer's. Again, this incident was reported in a paper. I was once stopping passers-by and asking them what they thought about MPs' salaries. Guess what, I stopped an MP. That appeared in *Punch*.

On the other hand, there's what might be called 'legitimate publicity'. This is when the press officer rings you up and says something like, '*Cosmopolitan* magazine want to interview you.'

You're quite free to refuse if you want, but I enjoy it. After all,

142

to work in TV you've got to be a bit of an exhibitionist, although I always find it surprising to be allowed to indulge this trait. Two of the longest interviews I've done were for women's magazines — *Annabel* and *Cosmopolitan*. They were conducted quite differently.

*Annabel* is produced by D. C. Thomson, the publishers of the *Sunday Post* and the *Beano*. It's a chatty, nicely produced magazine with nothing in it that could offend anyone's sensibilities, and seems to be aimed at young married women. The reporter from *Annabel* was a woman about my own age. She wanted to interview me at home and bring along a photographer to take a few shots of Cullen's Castle. This was all very alarming, as I hadn't washed the dishes for a week. So it was a clear choice between getting my hair done or picking the dirty washing off the living-room carpet before the photographer arrived. I decided to clean the flat; so much for glamour.

By the time *Annabel* knocked on the door I had as much energy as the various wet dish-cloths soaking in the kitchen sink — but the flat was sparkling clean. All except the bedroom, where I'd chucked the accumulated debris. *Annabel*'s photographer clutched a bottle of wine. I received this more gratefully than he knew and set to work with a corkscrew; then it was down to the serious business of being interviewed. What was worrying me was that everyone at the office would read whatever I said. Every day the press officer photocopies anything that's appeared about ITN in the press, and these copies are distributed round the building. Unwise remarks trot round after you for days. But *Annabel*'s questions weren't too bad:

'Why did you become a journalist?'

What I wanted to say was something about it being the only job I was offered when I left university. What I said, I thought, was that the ITN offer seemed too good to miss, as I had two brothers still being educated. What they said I said was that I'd been involved in student politics and edited the student paper. 'That combined experience attracted her towards television journalism.'

Then there was that impossible query: 'Why haven't you married?'

I was highly tempted to say, 'Nobody's asked me,' which in fact wouldn't have been quite true. I was under the impression that I'd said that things just hadn't worked out that way, but what I appear to have told *Annabel*, slightly to my shock, was, 'Many of the usual reasons for marrying don't exist for me. I'm as financially secure as anyone else with a good job.'

My feelings on reading that were as nothing beside my mum's.

More personal questions followed: if I did have any children, would I carry on working? Well, the real answer to that was: not unless I had to for financial reasons.

However, since the union at that time was fighting for decent maternity leave I felt that might be an undiplomatic disclosure, so muttered something noncommittal. What the magazine said I said was that I 'seemed quite confident' that I could combine marriage and children 'with a demanding career'. Mum didn't like that either.

We then came to the question of women in television getting the same breaks as the men. *Annabel*'s little tape recorder buzzed in an interested sort of fashion. This was clearly the core of the interview. At this time I still nurtured illusions about being allowed to do all sorts of interesting things like reporting on wars and famines, and had no intention of torpedoeing my chances. I regret to say that I sycophantically said that I thought women got just as good opportunities and I was sure that there was no discrimination. *Annabel* looked as if she didn't believe a word, then switched off the tape recorder to indicate that the interview was over.

'Very diplomatic,' she said. 'What's the truth?'

'What do you think?' I replied. She grinned and shook her head.

The article was very flattering and at least my mum liked the photos. In fact, these were a disaster. I'd posed against my bookcase — and among all the carefully planted books on economics and modern history was clearly visible a piece of literature which can only be described as explicit. Luckily, Mum had never heard of it, but everyone else I know had.

The *Cosmopolitan* interview was something else. *Cosmopolitan* is most definitely not aimed at the same audience as

*Annabel*: I think it's rather fun, but I'll read anything. *Cosmopolitan* were interviewing, or trying to interview, the whole batch of women reporters on national TV news. All six of us. My interview was conducted at a French restaurant opposite the Old Bailey. It's one of those establishments which is so French none of the waitresses speak English, so you can sit and listen to stockbrokers showing off the results of their holidays in the Dordogne. *Cosmopolitan* didn't speak French either so my 'A' level capacity managed to sound a good deal better than it really is. Reading Racine and Sartre for exams has left me able to curse fluently in French, or declaim expressively, but slightly at a loss when ordering a meal.

*Cosmopolitan* cut the cackle about husbands and ambitions and asked straight out if I thought women got a rough deal. Older and wiser by now, I told the truth: men get the big foreign stories while the women keep the home fires burning. Once she'd got what she wanted, she too turned off her tape recorder (not many people use shorthand these days — just baby cassettes) and we got down to some nice juicy gossip about our employers and salaries, and agreed that hard cash goes a long way to soothing injured feelings.

There's a lapse of several months between doing an interview like that and publication, and by the time the article was due to appear I was beginning to regret my frankness. I had visions of uncomfortable scenes in the Editor's office. I needn't have worried.

No one even remarked on my case for a stronger role for women reporters. They were far more interested in an anecdote about going on a pot-holing story and then being sent on to a Tory garden party to interview a Cabinet Minister. Because we'd been pot-holing I was in jeans and boots, wasn't carrying my police identification pass, and, what's more, we weren't in an ITN car, but were using a dormobile. It took half an hour to argue our way past the police on the gate. I'd kept this story rather quiet up till then. My colleagues weren't interested in boring women who want to go to war zones — but they laughed about the pot-holing story for days.

145

# 10

## A WELFARE STATE

Well, it's better to have people laugh at you than ignore you. Still, in some ways I envy the gossip columnists and suspect they have a relatively easy time of it. In the ordinary run of day-to-day news, you constantly, as a matter of pure routine, come across people who have to live with the most shattering problems.

When I'm knocking on the front door of a woman teacher sacked because she's unmarried and pregnant, or trying to interview a mother whose child has just died of bone marrow disease, I am frequently surprised how many people not only don't slam the door in my face, but are civil, friendly and try to oblige by giving a TV interview.

A few years back, there was a polio epidemic in Lancashire. I had come across the story purely by chance; there had been no great publicity.

I was news editing *News at One*, and a line came in from the Press Association saying there had been another suspected case of polio reported. That, said the PA, would make the eleventh in five months. I couldn't remember reading anything about polio cases, but eleven seemed rather a lot, so I took the press cuttings out of our library. There were a few short newspaper reports, but there did seem to be a gathering note of alarm. I showed the *News at One* Producer. 'Check it out,' he said.

I phoned the Department of Health press office.

'Yes, we rather wondered when somebody was going to ask about that,' said the press officer. 'We're getting very worried. People just aren't having their children vaccinated. We're going to put out a statement about it next week.'

The Department of Health weren't the only people worried. The news might not have had much impact in London, but round the Wigan area, where the outbreak was centred, people were falling over themselves to get vaccinated. Over twenty thousand people had rushed to vaccination centres and vaccine was having to be flown in from other parts of the country. Wigan seemed to be the appropriate place to start filming, so I phoned the local health authority for permission to film in a vaccination centre the following day, a Saturday, so that we'd have the film for *News at One* on the Monday.

Although the local health authority had said on the phone there were phenomenal queues for vaccination, once actually in Lancashire I began to have severe doubts about whether the queues would be quite so dramatic. Local officials do sometimes lay it on a bit thick when talking to reporters. So I phoned some cousins who lived in the Wigan area and deviously arranged that if, just in case, the queues weren't, as it were, my cousins would produce their own offspring to be vaccinated.

I was having anticipatory qualms as I drove to the health centre where I was meeting the film crew. Then I saw stretching a good hundred yards down the road a queue of about four hundred people, mostly women with small children. I had expected a couple of dozen at the very most.

I went into the building and introduced myself to the clinic doctor, then settled down to wait for the crew. They were a bit late, which was worrying, as I had also arranged with the local isolation hospital to film a boy who had been paralysed in his legs in this present epidemic. It had taken a great deal of diplomatic persuasion on the telephone to the child's consultant, a very formal gentleman, but the doctor had finally decided that the public did need to be warned, in the most vivid way, of the dangers of polio.

The consultant had approached the boy's parents; we felt this was a more tactful than an anonymous reporter ringing up. They had agreed willingly. However, the doctor had made it a condition that we film the child in hospital, and not at home, even though he was now well enough to live with his parents. I think the consultant felt that way he would have more control over proceedings. So we'd arranged for a taxi for the boy and his mum to take them to hospital. By now they'd be on their way and there was still no sign of the film crew.

Another half an hour ticked past. No crew. One of the clinic workers brought me a cup of tea. 'Your friends late, then?' she asked. She was a round, little grey-haired woman who looked like everybody's auntie.

I was becoming agitated, so phoned the office. 'Oh,' they said, 'we've taken them off your story.'

I choked into the teacup.

'There's been a murder nearby, so they've been switched to that.'

'Your friends not coming, then?' said the tealady kindly. 'And you come up all the way from London too.' She nodded her tight perm sympathetically.

I hastily phoned the consultant, in a horror of embarrassment, to try and explain what had happened. He was not in the least impressed by the story of the murder. 'We've taken a lot of trouble,' he said icily, 'to arrange this filming for you, involving a sick child. The least you can do is turn up.'

'Look, I am so sorry,' I said, trying to pacify his quite justified anger. 'Can we do the filming on Monday instead?'

'You will turn up?' asked the consultant warily.

'I swear,' I said, crossing my fingers. 'And of course we'll pay all transport costs for the child.' I hung up, sweating slightly.

'You in trouble, then?' asked the nice tealady. 'Have another cup, dear, you'll feel better.'

There was no vaccination clinic on Sunday, so we couldn't film that day and, just to complicate matters still further, I was supposed to be news editing on Monday morning, so I had to go back to London for that, then up to Wigan again straight after *News at One*.

Monday's vaccination clinic was in the evening. There was another long queue, even more dramatic in the dark, lit by television lights. The rush had accelerated with the confirmation of the suspected eleventh case. Polio had been virtually extinct in Britain for the previous fifteen years or so, but despite modern vaccination methods — no injection, just three drops of vaccine on a sugar lump — fewer and fewer parents were having their children vaccinated. We asked some of those queuing in a now persistent drizzle why they hadn't had their children vaccinated before.

'Never thought of it,' said one harassed looking woman, clutching an infant in arms, and with a couple of others in tow. She couldn't have been much more than twenty. Others had been worried because of the publicity surrounding the possible dangers of whooping cough vaccine and transferred their concern to the polio vaccine too.

This was precisely what the people at the Department of Health were now worried about. 'Do you realise,' the press officer had told me, 'that in some places over forty kids in every hundred haven't been vaccinated? That's nearly half the population. They've all forgotten what polio's like.'

The people queuing outside the clinic had been sharply reminded of the realities. But it was surprising how many thought they were going to have an injection. We heard snatches of conversation along the lines of: 'Will it hurt, Mum?' This from a tough-looking infant of about eight, the present terror of the primary school and a future Al Capone. 'No, pet. Just a little jab.'

Then, once inside, they took the sugar. 'Is that all, then, Nurse?' and went off looking a bit disappointed. They'd have nothing to brag about to their mates.

From the vaccination centre we went to the Monsall Isolation Hospital. It had turned out to be more convenient for all to do this bit of filming in the evening, when both the child's mother and doctor were free. The staff in the polio ward were very concerned at the continuing spread of the disease. The consultant welcomed us warmly, to my considerable relief, and waved away my renewed apologies for Saturday's mix-up. He had found some photos of the polio ward twenty years before. 'Look at that, lined with iron lungs. Patients in all of them — a life in an iron lung.' Now they had just one — unused.

'That, as much as anything else', said the consultant, 'illustrates the effects of vaccination.'

Then we met Simon. He had contracted polio early in the outbreak, in the autumn. He hadn't been vaccinated. He was a white-faced little boy of five who walked with a limp and wore calipers. 'He'll probably be crippled for life,' said the consultant. It was a disturbing and emotive picture, the little boy being examined by the doctor, and then limping off down the ward, his whole body swinging with the effort of walking. He was too young to be really aware of his disability.

'We had the others done,' said his mother, watching as he examined our camera with intelligent interest. 'But we thought we'd get him done when he went to school.' She was an unremarkable woman to look at, pleasant, nicely dressed, coping in a totally undramatic way with what must have been the most serious crisis of her life.

'Are you quite sure', I asked, 'that you don't mind this being shown on the news?'

She shook her head. She showed no obvious signs of distress. 'If it will get other women to have their children vaccinated, then it's worth it.' She spoke slowly as if she had thought it over. 'If it stops just one other child from getting what happened to our Simon.' She stood up and took her son's hand. Then they got into their taxi and went home.

'How bad is this epidemic really?' I asked the consultant, as much to break the sudden silence, as anything.

'Not good. That hot summer last year has made things worse. And you see, a lot of the parents themselves are too young to remember what polio's like. They've never seen a case. Another thing is that you do get the occasional adult coming back from holiday with it. In lots of foreign countries it's endemic.'

It's unusual to let your own emotions get very caught up in your stories, but before I left Lancashire, I rang my Wigan cousins. 'Did you ever get your brood vaccinated?'

'I haven't got round to it,' was the answer.

'Go and get it done,' I said in loud and uncompromising tones, thinking of my cousin's three children with an odd and uneasy chill.

Mind you, this business of practising what you preach can result in an undue number of painful experiences. A second vaccination campaign I reported was for German measles. Now, as most people, know, if a woman gets German measles during pregnancy, it can result in serious damage to her unborn child. She is then faced with the choice of an abortion or risking a damaged baby. So the Spastics Society were energetically pushing a campaign advising all women of child-bearing age to be vaccinated. I went off to film at a school where they were injecting a couple of classloads of girls.

All went well, until suddenly, right in the middle of filming, the doctor, a woman my own age, suddenly stopped, shooed the girls waiting their turn out of the room, turned to me and said, 'Have you been done?' Well, no, as a matter of fact I hadn't, but I'd definitely see to it some time.

'Now,' she said. 'Not some time. You either roll your sleeve up and get vaccinated or you stop filming and leave.'

'Stop laughing,' I said to the Cameraman as I unbuttoned my cuff. 'Film it.'

I forgot all about this incident, and a couple of days later had to have a batch of 'foreign travel' injections. I was supposed to be going to Thailand (though in the event I didn't, as the bank manager got a bit terse about my finances) so the jabs included one for cholera. Seven days later, I had a rash and was considerably under the weather.

'Never heard of cholera jabs doing that before,' said my GP rather worriedly. 'I think we'd better send you to the hospital for a check-up.'

151

As I left the surgery, his receptionist said, 'Oh, I did think it was good, you getting that German measles jab. I saw it on the box.'

'What German measles?' asked the GP, even more puzzled. I explained.

'Go away,' he said. 'What you have is a good old-fashioned case of German measles jab reaction. Nothing to worry about.'

'Does that mean I can have a couple of days off work?' I asked hopefully.

'No,' he said.

Sick children are constantly in the news. I suppose people feel it might so easily be one of their own kids that they identify with their problems. You do see some astonishing bravery. At least forty children a year die in this country of kidney failure, simply because there are neither the machines nor the specialist staff to treat them. Forty children; that's exactly half the eighty who develop kidney failure each year.

We went to film a teenager — call her Penny. Three times a week she had to spend eight hours a day linked to a kidney machine at her home in South London. 'She's lucky,' said her mother. 'She's alive, and she has a machine at home. No more treks up to the hospital.'

Penny was an exuberant young woman wearing a Capital Radio T-shirt. The Cameraman suggested she wear 'something a bit less commercial, dear', but she looked so disappointed, he relented.

'Can I listen to Capital while you're filming?' she asked, laughing a bit at herself. 'I always listen to them while I'm on the machine.'

She connected herself up expertly and showed us how she adjusted the controls. She kept asking us impossible questions like, 'How many elephants can you get in a Mini?', tossing back her shaggy black hair and shaking with giggles.

The machine draws blood from her body, cleans it, and then pumps it back in again. There's nothing hit or miss about the treatment; a child who's properly looked after has a ninety per cent chance of living a full life.

Penny sat on the bed, listening to pop music. A phone was just by her hand, essential in case anything should go wrong.

Other than the tubes, the wires, the dials, she insisted she was

152

'Just like every teenager. There's nothing to it,' she said, having another look at the dials on the machine. You could watch the blood flowing through the tubes attached to her arm.

'How do you feel?' I asked.

'Great. It's so marvellous having a machine at home. I just feel so much fitter.'

'Would you like a transplant?'

'Of course, but I've got to wait till they get a donor, and I've got to be really fit for the operation.'

Her father explained. 'Even with transplants, the machines are very important, because of the shortage of kidney donors.' He looked at me accusingly. I fished out my donor card and showed it with an air of injured innocence. 'They need staff, too. When Penny went to the hospital, there were people coming up from Dorset — that's three hours' drive — because there wasn't a machine unit nearer.'

As we left, Penny's dad waved a kidney fund box at us. We paid up, thankfully.

But doctors do appear to be getting more militant, more willing to agitate on TV and in the press to get what they want for their patients. It's quite a shock the first time a doctor says openly, 'My patients are dying because there's no money to treat them.' Unfortunately the message gets blunted when this is such a fact of life that the doctors are saying it every day.

However, few have taken such a dramatic step as one Birmingham consultant, who organised a public meeting to explain to his patients why some of them were having to wait years for treatment. With about six hundred thousand people on waiting lists throughout the country at that time, the British Medical Association, a body not generally given to inflationed rhetoric, was describing the situation as 'a scandal without parallel in any technically developed country'.

The consultant told us he had one hundred and twenty-seven people on his waiting list for orthopaedic surgery. As things were going, it would be thirty-six years before some of them got into hospital. He's everyone's image of a consultant, bony-faced, intense, and a bit tetchy as he showed us gloomily round the hospital.

'Short of beds, operating theatres, and staff,' he said, and

153

added, 'And you're too young to understand the problem.'

He was a very difficult man for a reporter to handle — suspicious of our motives, but wanting the publicity for his case that we could give. He'd expected about thirty people at his meeting in a church hall in Sutton Coldfield. In the event more than two hundred turned up. They arrived in wheelchairs, shuffling on crutches, supported by friends, some complaining and irritable, others embarrassingly diffident. Chairs had to be moved, camera tripods shifted, as old men on sticks tottered past. It looked like an Out Patients on a busy day. The consultant was cheered as he stood to speak.

'You have no industrial muscle,' he told them, looking round. 'You can't go on strike and threaten the government.'

Reporters scribbled, intent on their notebooks, but it took TV to capture the extraordinary quality of the occasion. Few of these people would die without the operations they needed. But they'd have to choose between pain and a life on analgesics.

A couple of local MPs perched on the edge of the stage, looking, interestingly enough, not at the speaker, but at his audience's reactions. The old, the sick and the lame still have votes.

But inevitably not all those little problems with the Health Service can be traced back to government ineptitude, tempting though this may be. Hospital strikes are a recurrent feature of the news scene.

The amount of freedom the media are allowed varies enormously between hospitals. In some a consultant will agree easily to let you film; he'll square it with the administration, there's no red tape, and you're in and out in half an hour while the patients hardly realise you've arrived. Hospitals are understandably reluctant to allow you to wander round upsetting patients, but the administration will usually lay on some sort of facility. They'll let you film one ward, talk to a couple of selected nurses and the occasional patient. It's unusual to be barred completely.

A St Bartholomews diabetes consultant organised an amazingly speedy trip in half an hour flat. At another hospital, which had better be nameless, it took two weeks of negotiating. We were supervised by six, yes six, administrators, plus two doctors.

All we wanted to film was their computer.

But these were uncontroversial stories. Strikes are another sackful of haddock.

When two unions, the Public Employees, and the Confederation of Health Service Employees, became involved in a pay dispute at a major teaching hospital, the press moved in. Administration staff were reassuring people that medical treatment was going on as usual, but the nurses were having to clean the wards, helped by patients. We arrived and duly filmed the picket line outside, then I trotted in to ask the administrator if we could do a quick bit of filming round the hospital.

'I'm sorry,' he said, unapologetically, twiching the lapel of his regulation three-piece suit.

I was a bit puzzled by this, so persisted. 'We really won't take long. Just a quick shot of a ward, and perhaps the kitchens.' He said he'd think about it. I hung around for another half-hour, worrying about my deadline. My Cameraman came in.

'The pickets told me they let Thames News in yesterday,' said he.

I returned to the attack; still no joy. Then he said, 'Well, the last time you were here your team were very disruptive.' I was taken aback.

'I mean you personally,' he went on.

'But I've never filmed here in my life,' I exclaimed.

'Yes, you have,' he said, staring at me blankly.

'I haven't,' I replied. This could clearly go on all day. 'I really have never filmed here before,' I insisted, mentally promising mayhem on whoever had left me this load of trouble. Finally we were okayed to do some very limited filming, so we dutifully took pictures of nurses washing floors, and a rather distant film of kids in the wards. The essential matter of getting something for the news was now complete. I felt I'd better sort out this blot on my reputation.

I went back to ITN's library, which keeps records of all stories and the reporters responsible, and searched through. As far as I could trace, no one had been within miles of the hospital for years. I phoned and pointed this out. 'So it couldn't have been anyone from here, and it certainly wasn't me.'

'Well,' I was told, 'there was a stroppy TV crew here a few months ago, and I recognise you.' Curiouser and curiouser.

Suddenly light broke; just like in the cartoons where a little light bulb switches on.

The stroppy crew couldn't have been anyone from ITN, because we'd have a record of it. 'But,' I said, 'you may well have seen me about. One of my best friends is one of your registrars.' There was a pause while I waited for this to sink in. 'And I usually have lunch with her every week.'

There was a faintly disbelieving silence at the other end, but there was no way he was going openly to admit he was wrong. Still, when I asked to film there a couple of weeks later, they were extremely nice about it.

My acquaintance with the registrar had obviously caused some slight problems with the pickets. I'd not been able to fathom this general unpopularity. So I shuffled off to see the shop steward, a porter with whom I'd often had a chat while waiting for my friend to finish with patients. I hastily explained that this was where he'd seen me before.

'Ah,' he said, 'I was wondering a bit. You really are from the TV news then.' I produced my press card. 'Well, you can get those anywhere,' he sneered. Fortunately, at this juncture the Medical Friend turned up to see how I was getting on.

'Bu — I'm so glad to see you,' I yelled. She looked taken aback by such enthusiasm.

'Tell him where I work,' I pleaded.

She looked puzzled. 'She's with ITN,' she told the shop steward.

'Oh, that's all right then,' he said happily. 'Do you want to interview me?' Which all goes to prove that in journalism you are guilty as hell until proved innocent.

Good news being no news, or at any rate not very often news, you do get to see an inordinate amount of the more painful side of life. If it's not hospitals, it's something else; housing, that other cornerstone of existence takes up a lot of time.

We still occasionally do faintly stricken stories about the horrors of living in the surviving tower blocks. Many have been demolished, but hundreds still stand. Liverpool City Council had one particularly embarrassing estate on their hands.

The three blocks were known as the 'Piggeries'; when they were built in 1965 they had been christened by the more romantic epithet of 'The Streets in the Sky'. Now they were the town planner's dream turned into a particularly vicious nightmare. I met the crew at the flats.

156

'Lock your car,' said the Cameraman wisely. 'They'll nick anything round here.'

We looked up at the blocks. They were so derelict, it was hardly possible to credit they had been built less than fifteen years before. Even the children's playground had been vandalised until it was just a tangle of rusted swings and odd bits of concrete. Yet a handful of people were still living here; waiting to be moved out.

'It'll cost a million quid for the council either to do them up, or pull them down,' I told the crew. 'The council are hopefully looking for someone to buy them for private development. The best offer so far is ten quid.'

'Bomb them,' said the Cameraman economically. We went on a little tour of exploration. Everything that could be smashed had been; every wall that could be covered in graffiti was; and all of the most obscene and unimaginative kind. We cautiously went inside one flat. The door was broken, floorboards split, all the windows smashed, the lavatory kicked to pieces. These had been designed as three-bedroomed homes for families with young children.

The lighting man was looking through the remains of a window. Suddenly he yelled, 'Didn't you lock your car?' We all raced back. The door had been forced and my radio was gone from the back seat. At a safe distance, about thirty yards away, some children stood on a wall clutching my radio and jeering. It seemed an appropriate moment to explore further. I'm too old to chase twelve-year-olds round a housing estate.

An open walkway on each floor, reached by stairs or lift, runs outside the flats, with doors leading off it. All the lifts were out of order. 'Even if they were working,' said the Cameraman, 'nothing would get me inside one. You could be stuck for hours.'

We staggered up the stairs, carrying the gear between us. By the tenth floor we were breathless and panting. We found an old woman sitting on the stairs for a breather, before she struggled up with her groceries to her home on the eleventh floor. We gave her a hand. She had sparse grey hair and wore carpet slippers.

Not all the flats were derelict inside. Along one passageway, littered with rubbish, broken glass, bits of cardboard, we found one surprise. The same couple had lived there since the block opened. Their flat was delightful with fitted carpets, matching curtains, elegantly and quite expensively furnished.

'Why haven't you moved?' Their lifestyle seemed so at odds with the exterior.

'We've been offered other council houses,' said the lady of the flat. She was about forty-five and wore a very smart beige jumper and matching slacks. Her dark hair was cut short, to fall neatly off her face. 'But we didn't like them. They offered us slums. Well, we've lived in one slum, and we don't want to move to another. We keep our flat nice. We deserve a nice house.'

After that, I decided to do a piece to camera from the eighth-floor balcony, with the crew filming from ground level. We didn't have a radio mike with us, so ran a sound cable right down the side of the flats. All the thieving little boys came and yelled at the Cameraman while he was filming, but he just smiled at them. As the sound was being recorded from the eighth floor, they could yell all they liked.

The blocks each cost three hundred thousand pounds to build. Liverpool is still paying off the interest on the debt at twenty-seven thousand pounds a year. Whatever happens to the Pig-geries in the end, it'll be the year 2001 before the city can heave a sigh of relief at having finished paying for them.

'I wonder if my insurance will pay for the radio,' I mused on the way back to the cars.

'Not a chance,' said the Cameraman.

'That's nothing,' said Current Bloke, as I described the flats. 'You should come down to St — 's one night.' He worked a couple of nights a week at a shelter for derelicts in the East End. It was a surprising activity for one who spent his professional life in three-piece pinstripe.

'I'm not sure,' I said cautiously, 'that I really want my social conscience any more awake than it is already.'

The conversation was taking place in a French restaurant next to the Opera House. My social conscience was already putting me off my dinner. Finally, I capitulated. Derelicts, or dossers, rarely get much TV coverage except for 'Good News' stories like 'Crisis at Christmas' when a charity puts them up and feeds them for a few days.

The hostel we went to is open all the year round. It smells

strongly of mingled sweat, vomit and disinfectant. I stood in the background, spreading bread with marge, while Current Bloke chatted to the inmates.

Suddenly one of them pulled a knife, and stood, swaying, holding it. He looked at the knife as if he were surprised and waved it at Current Bloke. I was terrified. Bloke just leaned over and took the knife. The minister who runs the hostel walked over unhurriedly.

'Now then, John,' he said quietly. 'What's all this?'

The man just stood there. He was wearing a very dirty grey suit and a filthy T-shirt. His hair was long and grey, his eyes very pale blue. He suddenly sat down on the floor.

The minister and Bloke took his arms and led him over to a bench against the wall. I left the margarine and went to listen. The man looked at Bloke very blankly, and said in a soft voice, 'Sorry, I don't really know you.' There was a pause. Bloke just nodded, but didn't say anything. 'I don't think we've met before.' His voice was educated and sounded as if he had a faint Tyneside accent. There was another pause. 'Could we talk? It sometimes helps to talk to someone. Could we go outside?' He wiped his mouth with his sleeve. 'I find it easier to talk outside than in here.' He was barely audible.

Bloke led him outside into the street. It was freezing cold, and around were blank factory walls. They sat on a step. I hung just behind them, listening. They sat there on the stone step for nearly two hours. They had not met before.

'I started drinking,' said John, 'when I was sixteen.' He shivered.

'Do you want to go in?'

'No. I joined up, you know. I stepped off the boat in Singapore and spent the next three and a half years in Changi. I started drinking heavily, you know, really heavily, after the war. God, I want a drink. I haven't had a drink for three hours. It's terrible when you're coming off it.'

'Do you want to give up?' asked Bloke.

'No! No, I don't want to give it up. It's lousy afterwards but it's great while it lasts. I was in a recovery unit for six weeks. I didn't have a drink for four weeks and then started drinking in secret. I've been on the white stuff [meths] today, got pretty tight. I'm

159

sixty-two. Do I look as if it's killing me?' He stretched out his hand. It was steady. 'Afterwards, for two or three days after a real bout, then I want to give it up. I was in Changi, you know. But I told you that. I'm a plasterer by trade. You know I was in Changi? You know a hundred years ago they had all the gin shops, they were all stoned out of their minds. But they managed to live and breed, didn't they? The marines used to have a ration of eight pints of wine a day. My mate, he got killed. We were in here and got settled. He decided he wanted some chips. I heard him go downstairs. Then there was a crash. I didn't think about it. I didn't see him for two days. I thought he'd got seven days. You know, in the slammer. Then the vicar here told me he was sorry to hear about it. "About what?" I asked. About Pete being killed. I didn't know. I'd been friends with him for eight years. The vicar said, "If that doesn't stop you drinking, nothing will." It just made me worse. I got eight pounds from the Social Security on Thursday. What I didn't drink went on the horses. I don't want to stop.'

He got up stiffly. 'I'm going in now.' He shook Bloke's hand and walked past me back into the hostel.

'Will he give it up?' I asked Bloke.

He shook his head. 'I doubt it. They very rarely do, and he doesn't want to. It's a worse prison for him than Changi ever was.'

# 11

## *HOLIDAYS*

'I really don't see why you need a holiday,' said Julie, with that especial candour which makes her so beloved by all her friends. 'After all, you never seem to do any work.'

We were sitting on the floor of my flat. I had bought a new living-room suite and disposed of the old one, rather precipitately as it turned out, because I'd been told it would be six weeks before the new suite took up residence.

'Leaving aside the question of whether I *need* the holiday or not,' I replied, 'may I remind you that it's my dinner you're eating, so lay off the abuse. Anyway, I'm totally exhausted.'

'Very nice too,' she said, her mouth full of pork chop. 'Why don't you buy a dining table?'

'I *have* bought a dining table. It's still at the warehouse. They can't deliver it for a fortnight.'

I lay on my back and contemplated the ceiling. I was getting used to living with no furniture other than a bed; there was a certain irresponsibility about it. 'Anyway, it seems a good time to go away. My friends are beginning to look askance at sitting on the carpet.' Julie thought about this for a moment.

'How are you for money?'

'Overdrawn by the amount of one living-room suite plus a dining table. In a word, broke.'

'So am I,' she said thoughtfully. Julie's job in market research involved a lot of jetting to glamorous hotels round the world, but surprisingly little in the way of hard cash. 'Why don't we go camping?'

We mused on this for a few moments. If nothing else has been made clear in the course of this narrative it should be obvious that Julie and I are essentially urban animals. 'Oddly enough,' I told her, 'I used to go camping quite a lot with my dad.'

'So did I,' she said. 'But that was fifteen years ago.' She examined her nail varnish carefully; it was a deep red gloss, called, I believe, 'Seductress'.

'What about your love life?' I asked. 'Is this the moment to abandon it?'

'Men,' said Julie. 'Huh.'

So, what with one thing and another, it seemed a good time to get out of London for a bit. And camping in a tent could hardly be worse than camping on the floor of my flat. We borrowed the tent from my brother, Jo, who accompanied his loan with dire warnings of the fate that would befall us if we didn't keep the guy ropes tight. Then there was the vexed question of transport.

'We could hire a Mini,' said I.

'You can borrow mine,' said Current Bloke. Julie and I stared at him, aghast at this evidence of mental instability.

'Are you sure?' I asked, feeling there was something faintly unethical about this, rather like taking sweets from a five-year-old.

162

'Why not? It's insured for all drivers. But Julie has to drive it, not you.'

This unchivalrous comment restored his generosity to its proper perspective. But while Current Bloke thought he was being astute in banning me from the driving seat, he had never actually seen Julie drive. She learned in Rio, and while she does have a British licence, there are times her motoring reverts to South American patterns. She used to carry a pistol in her glove compartment in Brazil.

'I think perhaps you should go away for a weekend, just to try it out,' said Current Bloke. He was visibly regretting his spontaneous offer. 'I mean, neither of you have been camping since you were kids.'

A week later we were beetling up the M1 heading for Wales. We had wanted to go to Brittany, but the Mini's owner had vetoed that firmly. 'Not in my car, you're not.'

Julie played little games of overtaking lorries all the way up. She hunched over the wheel, her hair — so blonde that only her best friends believe it isn't out of a bottle — flopping over her eyes, and experimented with seeing if she could get the needle to go right to the top of the speedometer.

'There's a seventy-mile limit,' I gasped, hanging on to my seat-belt as we overtook a Porsche, on the inside. 'And that's dangerous driving.'

She slowed to seventy. 'I didn't know Minis went that fast,' she exclaimed delightedly.

'I don't think British Leyland do either,' I muttered, feeling the sweat stream down my spine.

So it was perhaps not altogether surprising that five miles further on we were sitting on the hard shoulder waiting for the AA. Wisps of steam stole out from under the bonnet. 'Junk heap,' said Julie, kicking it gently with her snakeskin shoe. I felt this was a bit hard but said nothing, giving thanks for the unexpected reprieve. The car went to a garage to convalesce and we went back by train, staggering under the weight of tents, camping gaz stoves, sleeping bags and the like.

'So what are you going to do now?' asked Current Bloke, who was methodically working his way through the bottle of scotch I'd bought him as local anaesthetic before breaking the news.

'I think,' I said, 'I'll go to Crete. By myself.'

'But you've got no money.'

'I'm lunching with the bank manager tomorrow.'

My bank manager, for reasons best known to himself, took me to lunch at the Sporting Club, a gaming club. I would have thought one thing you don't do to customers with overdrafts is introduce them to still further ways of dissipating their well-earned. I pointed out this discrepancy.

'You don't gamble, do you?'

'How do you know?'

The result of this conversation was that I screwed another increase in my overdraft, for a holiday. 'Otherwise, I might take up gambling, and I didn't take that trip to Thailand, did I?'

It took only a couple of phone calls to arrange a flight to Crete. I'd first been there fifteen years before, and had returned frequently, although never before in the high season. It was depressing to note the changes; my favourite taverna outside Elounda had progressed from one table under a tree next to a wooden shack where meat was grilled on a makeshift barbecue to being a tourist spot. Now there were flocks of tables, wicker screens to keep out the sun, and menus in English. Everything was plastered with stickers from British and German travel firms.

Still, I thought as I strolled across the fields from the tourist village of Kritsa up to a ruined Byzantine city on a nearby hill, people are friendly. A bearded old man had waved and walked beside me for a while.

The walk, to the city of Lato, is optimistically described in the Berlitz guide book as 'forty-five minutes'. A German couple from my hotel had set out early wearing very proficient-looking walking kit. I passed them halfway up as they stopped to eat their sandwiches. The first part of the walk is through olive groves, then the track winds uphill over sparse fields grazed by scrappy-looking goats. The route is punctuated with roadside shrines. The last few hundred yards are over moorland, high and cold. Then suddenly the road stops, the hill falls over a cliff edge and the last few stones of the ancient city gleam, way below you. Inaccessible. I'm surprised no one has set up a tea and bun stand at the top.

I sat on a bit of marble and drank my Coke, tucking the can in my bag under the gaze of a bloke who turned out to be the Greek equivalent of the Department of the Environment. Then I started downhill. Halfway down, back in scrappy goat country, I met my elderly friend again. He gave me a bunch of flowers. He wore baggy black trousers and a very loose striped shirt. We walked on for a bit in what seemed at the time to be companionable silence. Then suddenly he made a determined grab at my blouse. I wasn't in any danger; he was about five foot two and I probably weighed a good stone and half more than he did. It was the shock. I stood and stared, then sprinted for the main road, where my bike was parked, covering the distance in about ten minutes. Once in safety I sat on a wall, panting in panic and surprise. I was still clutching the flowers. I dropped them. A woman came out of a house, bundled up in a black dress, looked at me, at the flowers, then at the way I had come. She pointed. Then she indicated a beard — like the old man's. I nodded. She roared with laughter and made the international sign meaning 'touched in the head'; I don't know whether she meant him or me. Then she picked up the flowers and went back inside, reappearing a moment later with a glass of retsina. As I sipped it she told the story to everyone who passed.

But she wouldn't take any money for the retsina and shook my hand warmly when I left. I looked back to see her standing waving until my motorbike turned the corner out of sight.

So, what with one thing and another, Crete was beginning to lose its appeal, and it seemed a good moment to contemplate options. I didn't fancy mainland Greece in June — not after my Athens excursion in pursuit of Miss Onassis. The nearest island, Rhodes, didn't, on the face of it, have much more to offer than Crete. I looked at a map. Egypt? Just how far were we from Egypt? I liked the idea of Egypt. A day trip to Egypt. It had a certain ring about it.

There was a boat on Tuesday from Iraklion to Alexandria. As the small vessel, Danish-owned, steamed into Iraklion harbour at dawn, I felt as if I had consciously stepped back thirty years; made that subtle jump between 'tourist' and 'traveller'. We're so used to hopping on a jet at Gatwick, and staggering off it three thousand miles away surfeited with gin, plastic meals and in-flight movies, that the leisured approach of the *Dana Sirena* into harbour had a curious element of novelty.

About thirty other people were embarking. We were a pretty motley collection including a couple of nuns, a clutch of Scandinavians in shorts and half a dozen English, all avoiding each other.

The ship, which had come from Venice, stayed in harbour a good half-hour before we were allowed on. 'Typical,' said one of the other Brits. 'They're just making us hang about.'

Then we were admitted, not up a companionway which had unrolled itself down the side, but into the car bay. Our luggage was whisked off, and we whisked after it.

For reasons of economy I had elected to share a two-berth cabin; fifteen pounds cheaper than having one to myself. I was banking on being left alone. The cabin was very small, with two bunks, a wash basin and a hanging cupboard. I sat on the bottom bunk till just before sailing, warding off any attempt to foist a companion on me. I got the place to myself.

It's a day and a night's journey to Alexandria, and there was simply nothing to do on board except eat, or drink at extortionate bar prices. There was a pocket-handkerchief swimming pool, full of squirming toddlers. I lazed on a deck chair, paid the extortionate bar prices and read *Frankenstein* in a state of blissful relaxation. It was so nice not to feel I *ought* to be doing something.

I'd struck up an acquaintance with a couple from Cheshire, both in their late twenties, blond and with a joint lopsided grin at the world. At first I'd taken them for brother and sister, especially as they were travelling with their in-laws in a large and boisterous family party. Bill and Anne stood beside me eyeing the harbour clinically. Conditioned by too many old movies, it was disappointing to see a modern — well, semi-modern — harbour.

The approach to Alexandria should have been romantic — shades of 'Quinquirimes of Nineveh' — now it's a quick hour from Cairo airport.

'Not what I'd expected,' said Anne.

She was a good seven months pregnant, and stood awkwardly, arching her back.

'What?' said Bill, photographing madly. I couldn't see much for the heat haze.

Bank officials came on board to change our currency to

Egyptian pounds. The currency used on the boat was Italian lire, but the Egyptian officials wouldn't change Italian lire. They would change anything else, but *not* Italian lire. There was a fifteen-minute queue to change money; nobody told the back of the queue the news about Italian lire. Bill, Anne and in-laws had travellers' cheques, I found a couple of sterling tenners.

Then we were all herded on to buses and sped towards Cairo. Every so often we passed large blue and white signs reading 'Foreigners are strictly forbidden to leave the main road'. There were occasional villages, glimpsed on the way, crude and muddy. This was the Nile delta and the road was bordered by a stream. A man was urinating in it peacefully.

'I'm glad we brought bottled water,' said Bill.

'Have you noticed,' said Anne, 'how every woman seems to be pregnant?' and patted her tummy. She drank some bottled water.

Cairo consisted of the usual tourist round including a quick peek at King Tut's treasures in the museum.

'I saw these in London,' said Bill, 'and a lot better displayed at that.'

The pyramids were a terrific disappointment. To eyes accustomed to tower blocks they seem insignificant, rather in the same way that mediaeval optical illusions don't fool modern vision. We shiftily eyed each other for confirmation of our disillusion.

'What price "curse of the pharaohs"?' asked Bill, breaking the mood.

It was killingly hot. 'I think I'll just sit down in the café at the bottom of the Sphinx,' said Anne. I went with her husband to climb the inside of one of the pyramids. You pay fifty pence or so and then wind in a long crocodile through a narrow passage. Next comes a steep plank of wood, running upwards through a shaft in the centre of the pyramid. There are little strips nailed across this for footholds and a constant stream of people clambers up in an ascending conga, surrounded by neat slabs of ancient masonry. The air is clammy and cold.

'Oh, Mummy,' I said as I slipped. Somebody laughed.

The climb took about ten minutes, stopping constantly to let people on the way down crush past.

'I don't fancy a fire in here,' muttered Bill, behind me.

When we finally got to the top we found a rectangular room with what looked like a topless altar at one end.

'Sarcophagus,' said the guide, immediately turning back. 'Now we go down again.'

This time it was our turn to push past the people going down. At the bottom the guide wouldn't let us out until we had paid another fifty pence for a 'tip'.

'Not much chance of refusing,' seethed Bill, paying up. A hundred sweaty people pushed behind us.

All the way down the short sandy road to the Sphinx, we were pursued by camel drivers, men with donkeys, and little boys selling iced drinks at twice the hotel rate.

By now we were late for the boat, so we all heaped back on board the buses. Our driver had, it transpired, a bet on with the others that he'd be first back to the harbour. First we overtook one bus, then they overtook us, then we overtook again causing an approaching car, tootling along legitimately on his own side of the road, to swerve off into the scrub. 'You see,' shouted the driver, 'I'm a great driver.' We hit a pot-hole, and bounced, before overtaking the next bus.

Anne was nervously eyeing her tummy. 'Much more of this and there'll be another little Egyptian.'

We overtook another bus, causing fresh screaming tyres. Drivers tended to head straight for us until they realised their nerve would break first. The sight of the *Dana Sirena*, rocking gently in Alexandria harbour, was quite a relief. Julie would have a wonderful time in a Mini in Egypt.

Anne's baby arrived two months later. 'Aren't I clever?' said her letter.

But my adventures in Egypt were as nothing beside those in its uneasy neighbour, Israel. I felt I should keep my politics in balance so, when I got the chance of a cheap package tour, I rang up the bank manager.

"I think it's my turn to take you to lunch,' I said sweetly.

'How much do you want?' he asked in a resigned voice.

I travelled with my little brother, Frank, all six foot of him. We timed our arrival in Tel Aviv in the middle of the worst storms for twenty years and spent the first night mopping up water from the floors of our rooms.

'This isn't rainwater,' groaned Frank. 'The sea's coming in the bedroom windows.'

I have never before been anywhere where people are so obsessed with matrimony. The first morning I was waiting in a bank to change some money. A girl ahead of me was displaying her engagement ring to the cashier. As she left, he turned to me, as if he'd known me for years.

'It's a terrible thing, she's only known him three months.'

'So?' I asked.

'Well, here you don't know who people are. You from England? Well, in England your mother knows someone, who knows their mother. That one, she doesn't know what she's getting.'

This was not the first time I had been taken for Jewish, but by the end of a few days in Israel, I was getting faintly tired of dealing with friendly enquiries like, 'Well, why don't you come and settle here? It's a good place for young people.'

The pièce de résistance came from the hotel owner, a sharp lad of thirty-odd of whom I'd have been wary even on home territory.

First day: 'This your first visit? You're not a tourist? Well, you don't look like a tourist.'

Second day: 'Are you free for dinner?' The answer to that was no.

Third day: 'We're having a little *chanuka* party here, can you come?'

Fourth day: Phones me in my room — 'Surely you're free tonight?'

'Look,' I said, 'I'm not into holiday romance.' On that cryptic remark he hung up.

After a week of this he finally collared me in the bar. 'It's a great place to live here,' he opened. 'This is my own hotel, you know. I'm not just the manager.' Long pause. 'My people are from New York.' Another long pause. Deep breath. 'You know, it's nice to meet an educated woman. There's lots of good jobs here for educated women. You been to college?'

I had begun to see where all this was leading, so just nodded, speechless with embarrassment. How could I explain I was not Jewish? And wouldn't that be a bit uncivil?

'What do you do? Oh well, there's lots of jobs here. You could

169

write for one of your London newspapers.' Another weighty silence. I finished my drink, wondering what to say to avoid hurting his feelings. 'Tell you what,' he said, 'why don't you come out for another holiday — on the house — in a couple of months. You could bring your mother. My mother lives in Tel Aviv.'

'Well, as a matter of fact,' I said, 'I've got what you might call a Bloke . . .'

'Oh.' Pause. 'Well, come anyway.' A lot less enthusiastically. He bought me another drink and slid off to his office.

Despite being cheated of a holiday romance I had a good time. There's a government operated tourist service called 'Egged' and we booked trips on their coaches. A popular T-shirt for sale in Jerusalem shows one of these buses, with the caption 'I saw Israel and lived'. We bought one for our brother Jo which read 'My brother and sister went to Israel and all I got was this lousy T-shirt'.

Jo wears the shirt for hang-gliding, under layers of pullovers, and it may have caused some sort of association of ideas because, a few months after my return from the Middle East, he appeared on my doorstep, displaying a newly acquired bright red beard and the T-shirt. 'I've got the hang-glider outside. Want to learn?' In a moment of aberration I agreed and, suitably kitted out in jeans and jumpers, got in the car. We decided to take Julie along too.

'Now,' he warned us, 'it takes weeks to learn to hang-glide. You have to learn from a proper instructor. It's not like the old days, you know, when idiots jumped off the top of cliffs.' Jo had just managed to get his hang-gliding licence, at the second attempt, and was clearly feeling a shade uppish.

'I've been hang-gliding before,' said Julie. Jo took his eyes of the road to stare.

'Don't tell me,' I moaned. 'In Rio.'

'How did you guess?'

'For a white slave, you seem to have got round a good deal.'

'I was working in market research then,' she said primly.

The hang-gliding was off a ridge perched in a waste of moorland. A dozen people stood around, eyeing each other's hanggliders with interest, and discussing the state of the wind.

'I came up here three times last week without getting a flight,' said Jo. 'The wind was too strong.'

The other hang-gliders all seemed to be wiry young men with beards and pipes — a sort of World War One fighter squadron clone. After a lot of what seemed to me aimless shuffling about and standing around drinking tea from thermos flasks, one of the men suddenly hopped over to his glider and attached it to his harness, then launched into space over the cliff edge. A few moments later he was above us, wheeling in wide, steady curves across the sky.

Jo stretched in a nonchalant fashion, which didn't fool me one bit. 'Think I'll have a go.'

He'd just bought a new glider, for five hundred pounds, and was dying to show off to his mates, let alone Julie, whom he'd been eyeing in a hopeful manner for the past few minutes.

A moment later he hurled himself off the cliff edge; he soared above us, then tilted and seemed to drop.

He's going for it,' said a Bearded Youth.

'What?' I asked, having visions of bearing the mangled remains home to Mum.

'Don't be silly,' said Julie. 'It just means he's going to try a long cross-country flight.' She got into deep technical conversation with the Bearded Biggles, comparing Rio technique to British.

'Oh dear,' said Biggles suddenly. I gazed cross-country to see Jo's black and orange glider floating gently down to the heather. It was about two miles away. 'He's lost the thermal,' Biggles explained to me kindly.

'Will he be okay?' I asked. After all, loony or not, he is my brother.

'Of course,' said Julie impatiently, as she and Biggles went off to look at his hang-glider. Not at all reassured, I watched Jo's fluttering glider settle, and then, through the binoculars one of Biggles' sidekicks handed me, saw Jo jumping up and down, trying to persuade a large sheep that his lovely plane wasn't for lunch. When he'd finally achieved that, he folded the glider into a long narrow bundle and heaved it on his shoulders.

'Shouldn't we drive down and pick him up?' I said. Nobody was listening. I turned just in time to see Julie take off with Biggles' glider. I hoped for his sake that her gliding was more conventional than her driving. Two hours later Jo appeared over the edge of the ridge, sweaty and bad tempered.

171

'I came out too soon,' he said. 'If I'd hung on, I'd have picked up another thermal.' He dumped the glider by the car, cursing gently.

'When do I get a go?' I'd sat patiently for hours.

'Oh, you'd have to have lessons and things about weather, and how gliders work. It's weeks before you can fly.' I couldn't think of a suitable response. Jo looked round.

'Where's Julie? I was going to ask her to dinner. So pretty and fragile, but able to hang-glide. What a girl.' He smiled dopily.

I grinned with sisterly malice. 'While you were showing off, one of your mates let her have a turn on his glider.' I paused to give this full effect. 'They've gone off somewhere. I told her I was sure you wouldn't mind. She said to thank you for a lovely day.'

'Oh,' said Jo despondently. He walked to the edge of the ridge and looked over it.

'Don't you think you're taking this a bit hard?' I inquired with barely suppressed glee. He kicked the turf, making quite a hole with his flying boots. The glider lay neglected by the car.

'Is there something special about hang-gliders that particularly attracts sheep?' I asked in an inconsequential fashion.

He shrugged gloomily.

'Why?'

'Another one's trying to eat yours'. He shrieked like a banshee and raced over to chase off the animal. He might fancy Julie; but he loves his glider.

172

# 12

## POLITICAL PARTIES

I had a kind of feeling that Jo was Well Out of It, but did periodically wonder just what Julie's evident appeal was; or, to be more exact, where I was missing out on things. Not, you understand, that I was exactly spending all my evenings at home, but Julie seemed to manage new variations on her love life each week. As she's a woman of positively aggressive virtue, combined with an alarming IQ, I found all this something of an enigma. The thing is, she *looks* like a dumb blonde, and a highly available one at that. Protective colouring, I suppose.

'Do you think', I asked her, 'that I could possibly have my Chinese dress back? You've had it a good six months.'

'Do you need it?' squeaked a startled voice at the other end of the phone.

'There's no need to sound so surprised,' said I, in what I hoped was a gently offended tone. 'In fact, I've got to go to the Tory conference, and it's always worth taking a halfway-smart dress. All those Young Conservatives, you know.'

'Are you a Tory?'

'What's that got to do with it? Anyway, there's a sort of ITN party one night, and we're expected to look tidy and not let the side down.

There was a pause, one of those ominous sorts of pause. 'Sarah?'

'Yes?'

'I got toothpaste on it.'

'You did what? How?'

'I cleaned my teeth in it. How else?'

'The noise you can hear,' I said, 'is me tearing out handfuls of hair. Go on.'

'Well, I've had it dry-cleaned once, and they can't get it out.' A long, long pause. 'I've taken it to an awfully expensive cleaners and they say they can do it, but not for a couple of weeks.'

'Oh,' I said. I mean what can you say?

'I'm sorry,' whispered a limp little voice. 'I didn't think you'd need it so soon.'

'Forget it,' I replied. 'On a more cheerful note, how's your love life?'

'Ahhhhh,' said Julie, and proceeded to tell me. At length.

'I thought you were off men?'

'This one's different. He's lovely. He's rich too,' she added as an afterthought.

'He has my sympathy,' I said, and rang off before Julie could ask what I meant.

I had to pack my suitcase for the Tory conference.

Forget anything you have ever heard about the glamour of a party conference, in which all-enveloping title I include the TUC. They're a kind of treadmill of hard work for the journalists covering them. And the lower down the journalistic scale, the harder the sweat. My humble role at a large number of these occasions was to log what the speakers were saying — every single speaker.

Party conferences are recorded by TV cameras in the conference hall. The actual image, the picture, is relayed the whole way back to London, where it is recorded on videotape machines. While the political correspondents in, say, Blackpool might say, 'We'll take that bit of Mrs Thatcher, where she's talking about prices,' writers in London have got to be able to find that part of the speech among about eight hours of conference proceedings.

So with all this day-long political waffle, interrupted by rare golden nuggets, someone has to take detailed notes of the lot, and record the exact times against each paragraph. Otherwise, in the hours and hours of videotape, no one would be able to find anything.

The writers sit near the camera, on the balcony of the hall. Besides their notebook they have a clock in front of them synchronised with the Post Office recorded TIM time. As the actual proceedings are recorded in London, the correspondents also use a tape recorder to remind themselves exactly what has been said.

A typical writer's 'log' looks something like this: Joe Bloggs speaking:

11.33   Inflation curse of Britain today (Tape 8/232)
11.35   Government must resign      (8/239)
11.37   Forward to new unity       (8/248)

Behind the writer sits the correspondent making a note of anything that catches his attention.

When the time comes to select the speeches that will be used, the discussion goes something like this:

'Who was that bloke with the beard, the one from Wigan? No, not the one with glasses, the other one,' says the Producer.

'No, no. The councillor. That one.'

'Good point that about inflation,' says the Correspondent.

'Don't you mean MLR?' says someone. 'Or do I mean M/3?'

'No, no. It *was* inflation. Anyway, isn't that the same thing as M/3?'

'Let's hear it,' says the Producer.

The writer should then, in theory at any rate, be able to look back through the day's log and say, 'Joe Bloggs, real time 11.33, tape eight at 232,' and be able to find the spot on the tape to replay it to the Producer and Correspondent.

Then the Producer says, 'Let's take a bit of that, but pick it up later, where he says the government should quit.'

So the writer gets on the phone to his opposite number in London.

'Okay another bit on inflation. They want to pick it up at 11.35 and ten seconds where Joe Bloggs says, "This government, the worst . . ." Got that?'

'Okay,' says London.

'Yes, and end it at "a newly united Britain". It should run about twenty-five seconds.'

When the Correspondent and Producer between them have selected the various bites they want from the day's proceedings, the Correspondent writes a script linking them. Then he either appears live, from Blackpool, introducing each speaker, with that speaker being played in from London, or he prerecords his links. They are recorded in London, and London then edits the whole lot together.

When everything is going live, the Director in Blackpool and the Director in London can talk to each other over a sound link. And although the Correspondent is in Blackpool, he is cued to start and stop speaking by the Director in London — just as though he were sitting in ITN Studio One.

'Okay, Mike, ten seconds to you,' says London.

'Ten, nine, eight . . .' Then the floor manager in Blackpool drops her hand and Mike begins.

ITN manage this operation with a clutch of technical staff, a director, a floor manager, a PA, two or three writers, a producer and a couple of correspondents. By the end of the week, all are half a stone lighter and considerably the worse for wear.

Usually the writers take it in turns to log the speeches, trot round to the makeshift ITN office (non-soundproof plasterboard) to fish out the good bits on tape, and have a quick cup of coffee. But, on one memorable occasion, most of the team were attacked by an unusually virulent gastric flu bug within hours of arriving at Blackpool. One secretary was so ill she was dispatched home. A writer collapsed writhing whitely and was taken to bed. That left two of us standing (just), apart from the two correspondents, and they didn't look too good either.

176

Between the two of us we sort of added up to one writer. My colleague had a dizzy head and couldn't write, but she could walk around. I couldn't even stand up without being horribly sick, but I could still write, after a fashion. For three days I stayed pinned to my chair in the conference hall, while Colleague shuffled to and fro with tapes and notes looking like an animated ghost. She was also chief sub, a kind of Deputy Producer, on conference inserts, a role she fulfilled in a haze of kaolin and morphine. Luckily the Producer was okay, so tore around dispensing brilliance and sympathy.

Despite such occasional misfortunes, conferences are a definite change. They're usually held in Blackpool or Brighton, though the Liberals opt for quieter places like Llandudno. Blackpool is fun. With the illuminations up, and the pavements slicked by rain, Blackpool definitely has something. A favourite spot for lunch is Yate's Wine Lodge, a spit and sawdust establishment which sells champagne by the glass, and barm cakes. It's an echoing place, all bare boards and local biddies eyeing this influx from the south with acute, and possibly well-justified, suspicion. For a couple of weeks a year a horrific London mob washes through. Then the pub settles to its usual riotous calm.

The food in Blackpool tends to be good. Just behind the imposing Imperial Hotel is a traditional fish and chip shop, much patronised by telly types. We had forcibly to drag a Very Senior Correspondent out of there one night to do his bit on *News at Ten*. 'But I want a banana fritter . . .' he kept saying plaintively.

But there are also classical fish restaurants which can rival some of the best in London, lurking above unpretentious chippies, and a good Italian place hiding behind a Victorian villa façade. There's also a place on the front that isn't licensed but sells oysters and seafood with thin brown bread and butter. Tea comes in blue willow pattern. I'd always been rather partial to this shack until I turned up there once, not in a recognisable TV group but with Current Bloke, who was in Blackpool on business.

We asked for oysters. They were slammed down in front of us.

'Could we have some brown bread?' asked Current Bloke.

'You should have said before,' grumbled the waiter.

The bread and butter arrived as we were finishing. 'Well, you'll still have to pay for it,' said the waiter.

177

'Pot of tea?' I asked.

'We're closing,' he said.

'I thought you said they were good,' said Current Bloke.

'Well, they are, if you've got a newscaster in tow,' I replied gloomily. And then they wonder why people go to Benidorm. Now Brighton is totally unimpressed by telly ephemera. It's nicer being a nobody in Brighton than in Blackpool. On the other hand, it's harder to get a quick bite because you've got to get back to the conference hall to carry on with that interminable logging.

At these events, dominated by the TV image of politicians, the real politicians trot past, pale and tired, clutching bundles of conference agenda and staring into space with deeply abstracted expressions as if afraid they won't be recognised. What you might call recognisable politicians frequently nod to absolutely everybody, and say 'hello' for fear of offending somebody they were introduced to back in '64. Some seem genuinely to enjoy the occasion as a chance to take the media for a ride, and accept a lot of expensive drinks, while saying nothing immediately to the purpose. And there are the little huddles in corners of the cocktail bars which suddenly go quiet if anyone approaches.

And, of course, there's the problem of trying to sleep. Lots of padding footsteps and strangled giggles in the corridor outside your hotel room. You'd wonder where they get the energy from. For reasons which totally escape me, the transit activity always seems to be worse at the TUC and Tory conferences. Because of the sheer numbers of conference delegates and journalists, all the hotels are packed; even small groups from one constituency may be split over several hotels, possibly nine miles apart. So at dawn the taxis start a general all-change. You'll be woken by the roar of a taxi engine under your window, and a quick peek displays a rumpled form catapulting from the taxi to the hotel. Half an hour later, bathed, shaved and serious, the form will be sitting at breakfast, innocent as a boiled egg, contemplating the front page of the *Telegraph* or *Morning Star*, depending on the political nature of the occasion.

Interestingly, conference hotels, indeed all big business hotels, seem to have an extraordinary kind of twenty-four-hour existence. There's always a group sitting in the corner of the lounge talking earnestly over a briefcase of papers and a heap of cigarette ends. This all-night consciousness was illuminated during a brief stay at a larger and more modern Midland hotel.

I'd checked in rather late, with no luggage other than a briefcase and a couple of cans of film. I intended to get an early train to London and have the film processed back at base in time for *News at One*. By midnight I was tucked up in bed and sleeping happily.

I woke thinking the phone was ringing. No. But there was a loud and persistent bell going in the corridor. I sat frozen for a moment before I realised. A fire alarm. Now, I'm one of those people who always notes fire exits and so forth, and believe firmly in the principle of not stopping to put on lipstick, but running like hell.

I grabbed the bits and pieces I distinguish with the title of jewellery and the ITN film cans, and tore out of the room, still buttoning up my dress, barefoot, dishevelled, and in no state of mind to worry about it. As I cannoned through the fire door, I fell over a bloke still struggling with his trousers and displaying more of his marriage prospects than is customary in hotel corridors.

'Excuse me,' he said, blushing in places I wouldn't have thought it possible.

'Think nothing of it,' I yelled, running down the stairs. The fire doors led out on to a patio in front of the hotel and half a dozen equally undressed people tumbled on to it. We stood around and looked at each other. There were no signs of fire, no engines, nobody from the hotel staff checking that people had escaped. The bloke with the trousers, bare-chested and shivering, looked round.

'Odd,' he said.

The hotel, a modern skyscraper, towered above us. We padded barefoot across the concrete and peered into the hotel lobby. It was sprinkled with men and women, all wearing the usual amount of clothing and looking unconcerned.

We went in; another guest eyed our dishevelled entrance. 'That's the third alarm they've had today,' he said. 'There's something wrong with it.'

The Bloke with the trousers, six foot five of angry Glaswegian, stormed across to the desk. 'Well, what's your explanation?' he asked.

'I'm not going to apologise,' replied the manager, blinking

179

blond rabbit eyelashes. 'After all, it's better that the bell is working.'

He moved in a miasma of aftershave, presumably to compensate for a lack of chin.

'And what,' I asked, 'are we supposed to do if the alarm goes off again at three o'clock?' He shrugged.

I gave up and trotted over to the lift. A few people eyed me curiously. As I got out of the lift, a mother, father and their two children, neatly washed, brushed and coated, were waiting to get in.

'Is there a fire?' they asked.

'No,' I said.

'Oh dear, and we got the children up.'

They sounded quite regretful.

'Well, if there had been a fire you'd all have been barbecued by now,' I said rather sharply. 'You shouldn't go by lift.'

'Now, don't you speak to me like that,' said Dad, turning puce.

I ignored this and plodded back to my room.

I was no sooner neatly disposed back in bed when I realised my watch was missing. It was undoubtedly my most valuable possession, an inheritance from a much-loved relative. So it had enormous sentimental value as well.

I tried to ring the porter. After a dozen attempts I got through and reported the loss. Then once more I got dressed and started to look for it. No sign. Back down to the lobby.

'Can I see the manager?'

He duly appeared, presaged by a renewed blast of perfume and I explained that my watch was missing, either dropped in the scramble for safety, or pinched while I was out of the room.

'Why didn't you report this at once?'

'I *did*, to the porter.'

The porter was summoned. 'It's not my job to look for watches,' he said.

'Why didn't you tell me about it?' the manager answered, rubbing where his jaw bone should have been.

'Not my job.' He went off.

'Well, I'm very sorry about your watch, dear. But it was insured wasn't it? So why fuss?'

'I want the police called.'

'Police? What for, dear? Just for a watch?'

I took a deep breath. 'It was my watch, not yours. If you don't call the police I will. And the local papers for seconds.' This was something of a bluff.

He was gratifyingly startled. 'Are you sure it's not in your room?'

Well, of course I was sure, but he dispatched a large and competent lady, the swimming instructor by day, just to make sure I hadn't hidden it in my washbag. While she did that, he and I scoured the fire escape and all the surrounding area. Ten minutes later the police arrived.

They came up to my room and took the details, then went off to do a bit more searching. They came back and took still more details.

'Have a drink,' I offered.

'Don't mind at all, miss,' said the elder one, rubbing his hands. He took off his cap. 'Hot in here.'

They had a couple of beers from the self-service fridge in the room. It was that sort of hotel. I made a mental note to make sure the hotel paid for those drinks. Then they left, making a lot of soothing noises. Finally, at nearly four o'clock I got to bed.

The watch, of course, never turned up. And the hotel wouldn't pay. 'Not our fault,' was the parrot cry. How any establishment which has a dotty fire alarm can expect return custom, I'll never know.

On the train back to London, leisurely eating a British Rail sausage, I realised that the man sitting diagonally opposite was trying to catch my eye. I raised the ever useful eyebrow.

'Last night . . .' he said; everyone in earshot stopped eating to listen. 'Did you get to bed okay?' he continued. The silence in the restaurant car was broken only by the rustle of *The Times* from someone who must have been hard of hearing.

'I don't suppose you recognise me with my clothes on,' he said blithely. Then stopped and went an entertaining shade of pink. An elderly man in a pin-striped suit next to me cleared his throat and became suddenly very interested in the label on the marmalade jar. A younger type sitting next to my nocturnal friend, choked into his table napkin.

'More coffee, madam?' asked the British Rail steward, equally pinioned by the tale of lurid drama and passion that was clearly about to unfold.

'Funny things, fire alarms,' said my Friend, thereby making the situation even worse.

We were still trying to explain to passengers sitting nearby when the train pulled into Euston. I don't for one minute think any of them believed a word of it.

# 13

## *WALKABOUT*

But party conferences and smart hotels are but a brief twitch in
the reporter's year. For the general reporter, as opposed to the
political corespondent, the most frequent contact with high-level
politics is that form of human activity known as 'doorstepping'.

'Sarah,' says the News Editor, 'we think Callaghan's going to
resign today. Go down to Number Ten, and see what you can
get.'

This statement requires translation. If a PM resigns, they will give our Political Editor an interview later in the day. The Political Editor will be given regular briefings from Number Ten about what's going on. What the News Editor means is that you go down to Number Ten, hang about in the rain, and if and when Mr Prime Minister appears, yell something like 'Mr So and So, are you . . .' which is about as far as you'll get before he gets into the car and shuts the door.

There's a little white line painted on the pavement outside Number Ten, and reporters and cameramen have to keep to one side of it, otherwise the police get annoyed. So there's no question of standing in front of a PM so they can't get past you and have to talk to you, a technique often employed with lesser mortals.

I seem to have spent a disproportionate slice of my working life standing behind that little white line.

As a variant on 'doorstepping outside Number Ten' there's the 'Go down to London airport' routine. Let's say the Foreign Secretary has been having talks in Washington, the News Desk line goes 'Go down to the airport and see if he'll say anything. His plane gets in seven thirty tomorrow morning.' Now there will, of course, be a press briefing later in the day, but that doesn't matter — you've still got to go down to the airport. When you arrive, at seven fifteen, the first thing to do is to check that the flight from Washington is still due in on time. Then you go round to what's called the press conference room. This is in Terminal Three, just past the cafeteria and through a Staff Only door. It's a large room littered with chairs and tables and there you will find your crew, a clutch of reporters, and possibly the BBC.

Senior politicians do not, of course, just walk through the Flight Arrivals channel like anyone else. They come through the VIP suite. From the press conference room you can watch through a locked glass door as your quarry walks into the VIP suite, where he'll have a nice cup of coffee before being whisked back to London by car. You ask the London airport press officer if she'll ask the politician to come and have a word with you. She goes off, to return five minutes later shaking her head, just as you thought she would.

You phone the office. 'He won't talk.'

'Why not?' asks the News Desk.

'He went out through the VIP suite.'

'Oh. Well, did you ask if he'd talk?'

'Of course.'

'Oh well, it doesn't matter anyway, the Political Editor's interviewing him this afternoon.'

Then you go and have a cup of coffee and exchange grumbles with your opposite number from the BBC who's been having an identical conversation with his own office.

On one occasion I was at the airport with another of our reporters, Clark Kent, with whom I'd not worked since the Blunt affair. It was at the beginning of the Iran/Iraq crisis, and we were trying to find anyone who'd flown in from Iraq via Kuwait. All the long-distance flight arrivals, other than VIPs, walk from customs and immigration through the same door. The only way to find where they've come from is to ask. All of them. We knew a flight from Kuwait had just landed, but so had flights from Hong Kong, Canada and all stations east and west.

Clark Kent stood on one side of the gangway, me on the other.

'Excuse me, have you just arrived from Kuwait?'

This usually resulted in puzzled looks, an occasional 'Why?' and for some inexplicable reason the frequent proud rejoinder, 'No, Seattle.'

A few people looked excessively shifty. 'Do you think,' I asked Clark, 'they suspect we're a final customs check?'

'Not me,' he said, waving a clipboard emblazoned ITN, though what that would mean to a smuggler from Seattle is anyone's guess.

I bore down on an inoffensive-looking bloke. 'Excuse me . . .' Clark was jumping up and down behind him gesticulating madly. I ignored this. 'Excuse me, have you come from Kuwait?'

The bloke looked baffled, shook his head and strode off, grinning. Clark came over.

'You twit.'

'What?'

'That', he said witheringly, 'was Donovan.'

'Who?'

'The singer.' He threw his hands in the air. 'The folk singer.'

'Oh.'

Ten minutes later he sidled across sheepishly. 'You know what

I've just done?' I raised an enquiring eyebrow. 'That bird who's the star of *Bride of the Vampire* on the telly. Over here to promote a film. I just asked *her* if she was in from Kuwait.'

The only person who did arrive from Iraq via Kuwait that morning changed planes at Amsterdam and arrived at Terminal One. We had another reporter there, but the man wouldn't talk anyway.

Another job which is more or less routine is the 'walkabout'. I always thought that term originally denoted someone pushing off into the bush for a few months to commune with nature in peace and quiet. Well, the riot of a political walkabout is the exact antithesis of that. I think the word 'walkabout' must be the only one in English which means one thing and its exact opposite.

'Anything for me tomorrow?' I asked the News Editor with my usual lack of guile.

'Yes, as a matter of fact, rather a nice little story. The Prime Minister's going to open a children's nursery centre in the East End. All the cash has been raised voluntarily.'

'Any kids going to be there?'

'Mmm, yes, that's what makes it appealing. There'll be a demo too, so it won't be too sugary. If you get a chance, ask her if she thinks the unemployed should be helping with schemes like this.'

The PM was due to arrive at ten o'clock. By quarter past nine most of the press had already assembled. The playschool was in a prefab-type structure, tucked away on a patch of former wasteland, behind some buildings. The only way to get to it was by a gate from the main road. A handful of demonstrators had already turned up, and stood by the gate looking bored.

'What's happening?' I asked a girl with a Nikon camera slung round her neck; people with Nikons hanging round at events like this tend to be press photographers.

'They won't let us in,' she said.

'Where are you from?' She named a left-wing magazine.

'Haven't you got a Met press pass?' She shrugged.

I walked up to the two police on the gate who'd been eyeing this exchange, and produced my press card. Although our union, the NUJ, issues press cards, the Metropolitan Police issue their own, and don't accept the NUJ card. I showed my Met card, and was allowed in.

'Can we park our cars inside?' asked the Cameraman.

'Why?'

'Well, it's all our gear, lights and things.'

'You can bring the cars in to unload your stuff, but then you'll have to park somewhere else.'

'But there's masses of space.'

'Sorry mate, orders.'

I left the crew arguing the toss with the law and went to have a look at the playschool. Inside it was bare, except for some paintings on the wall, a table with some paints on it and a few toys scattered around rather forlornly.

'Mornin', darlin'.' The *Evening Standard* suddenly popped out of the woodwork, festooned with cameras and light meters. With his usual grasp of the real priorities, he'd managed to find himself some coffee.

'Where'd you get that?' I indicated his cup.

'Ah, you're just a minute too late, they're all getting ready for The VIPs now. Have a drink of mine.' He passed over the cup.

'There seem to be rather a lot of people here.' There were at least fifty press hanging about. Our lights man was deep in conversation with his oppo from the BBC deciding to pool resources.

'You wait till the kids get here,' said the *Standard*, with relish. 'They're bussing seventy-five in to meet the PM.'

'That's good,' I said. 'It'll make a very nice picture.'

'If you can get it,' said the *Standard*, who was clearly feeling more misanthropic than usual. 'There are about two hundred dignitaries coming along as well.' He pushed his hair out of his eyes.

I looked round the room, which suddenly seemed tiny. 'Are they all coming in here?' I squeaked.

'Looks like it.' He leaned against the wall, the picture of a man without a care in the world. 'I think', he continued, 'it's going to be a bit of a scrum.' There was a Dennis the Menace badge in his lapel.

'Did you know', I enquired, 'that your accent gets about three times more Irish when you're trying to wind somebody up?'

'Now would I do a thing like that?' he asked, in an improbable brogue.

I ignored this, and went outside again to try and find out what was going on. Beyond the gate more demonstrators had collected and were enthusiastically chanting 'Right to Work'.

About a hundred guests milled around wondering what to do. The ladies favoured aggressively well-tailored suits, their men in matching male attire. In the middle of all this a Franscican friar was having an animated conversation about remedial education with a couple of policemen.

The organisers were trying to get people to stand in some kind of a line, without a great deal of success. My Cameraman materialised.

'Hold this, will you.'

'This' was a spare mag for the camera. The standard mag holds four hundred feet of film, ten minutes' worth. That's usually enough for a short story but it's safe to have a spare. We positioned ourselves by the door of the playcentre to wait for the PM.

A few minutes later the car drew up, to muted applause from the invited guests. Then a demonstrator, who'd slipped somehow past the police, pelted up.

'What are you doing about the f...ing unemployed then?' she yelled. The PM murmured something polite and walked on; the demonstrator was hauled off.

'I do so wish', sighed the BBC in my ear, 'they wouldn't use words like that. It does make editing unnecessarily difficult.'

This incident triggered a kind of general rush. As the PM walked to the door all the dignitaries broke ranks and pushed after her. Luckily my crew and the BBC had got in just ahead, but I was pinned back in the scrum. Just to complicate matters the swing doors managed to work loose and swing back, and the people trying to fix them got pushed over by the advancing hordes. I abandoned my manners and shoved hard through the crowd to reach my crew. The Cameraman was balancing unsteadily on one of those tiny little nursery school chairs, filming over people's heads. The PM was being presented with flowers by a little moppet, who didn't seem at all bothered by the crush. When the PM bent to have a chat with the toddler, we took the opportunity to have a quick chat about tactics.

'This is bloody terrible,' said the Cameraman. 'Can't you get the organisers to hold people back a bit?'

'Well, they said they'd try, but I think it's got past that.'

We looked around. At a table further along, not yet mobbed, some handicapped children were playing with paints.

'I'll go and fix myself there,' said the Cameraman. 'She's bound to talk to them, so we'll get one complete sequence, then I'll just have to scramble what I can. You stand behind me, and try to stop people pushing me over.'

The PM, as predicted, then walked across to the table and looked at the paintings. She began to show one of the children how to build a tower of bricks. Our cameraman was kneeling just behind her, filming away like mad. The Prime Minister and the children seemed the only beings who were totally unflustered. I felt someone tugging my arm, and heaved myself out of the crowd. The BBC reporter was standing on the fringe of the mob, rivalling the PM's equanimity.

'Are you going to try and talk to her?'

'Well, that's the general idea.'

'About unemployment?'

'That and other things. Have you seen her press officer?'

We finally hauled the PM's press officer from the heap. His natty Savile Row suit looked distinctly crumpled, his tie was askew and what remained of his hair was drooping over his forehead.

'What about a quick chat then?' we asked, adding to his worries.

'I don't think so. What do you want to ask her?'

'Oh, just about how this unit was built from private funds, and is that the sort of thing she wants to see more of?' said the BBC blandly.

'I don't know, I'll tell you later on.' He vanished into the scrum again.

The *Evening Standard* surfaced. 'What a mess. She's going outside next. I'm going to try and get in position there.' He struggled off to the door. I stood on a chair to try and see my crew. They had stuck right beside the action and seemed to be in a good position. Someone I didn't know came up to me. 'Have you got any of the facts and figures? I got here late.' This kind of information sharing is quite common on routine stories, especially when someone arrives late. It's a mutual insurance policy. I looked at my notebook.

'Yes, it cost eighty thousand quid, all raised by charity, Royal Variety Club, I think, put up a lot of it. They'll have a hundred and fifty kids a day, handicapped as well as healthy.'

'Thanks,' he said, taking it all down. I fought my way back to the crew.

'I think we've got enough here,' said the Cameraman easing himself out of the crush.

'What about sound?' I asked. In that sort of scramble you might get the pictures but sometimes don't pick up the chat — and of course we wanted to hear the PM talking to the children.

'Okay, I think,' said the Sound Man. 'I was in very close.'

'Shall we get a bit outside?' I asked.

'Well, we've got enough, really. Well, okay, why not?'

Outside, there were some children in wheelchairs. The playground wasn't finished, so there was just a narrow strip of flagstones, the rest was rough ground and very muddy. This deterred some of the onlookers so we got some relatively calm filming. Then back inside for the formal opening, and a few little speeches.

The BBC and I went to look for the press officer again.

'Okay,' he said. 'You can ask her just three questions.'

'Each?' I asked.

'No, between you. You'll have to work it out. And *nothing* on unemployment.'

We took our respective film crews and went to wait by the PM's car. A number of other reporters, who hadn't been involved in these negotiations, tacked on behind us. The Prime Minister came out and prepared to answer the questions; I was trying to work out a way of asking if she expected the unemployed to help in centres like this one, without actually using the word unemployed. The BBC asked a couple of questions, then someone from radio jumped in. I could see the press officer making signs to us to stop the interview. Not before I get my sixpence worth, I thought.

'Madam Prime Minister' — I was having difficulty phrasing it — 'It's all very well for fairly well off people, like the Variety Club, who can afford to cough up money. . .' Someone thumped me in my ribs. I stumbled and gasped inelegantly.

'Yes,' she replied, ignoring the radio man who was trying to get a word in. 'Go on.'

'Well, what about ordinary people, you know, with money short all round?' The PM's answer could have been straight from the pages of the nineteenth-century's Liberal economists, about how people could help with the electrics, painting, and so forth. People didn't have to give money, they could give time. Then it was into her car and away.

'Well, I got what I wanted in the end,' I said to the crew.

'We ran out of film on the answer,' said the Cameraman gloomily.

'What?'

'Well, that's why I tapped you on the ribs, to let you know.'

'You mean we've lost all that Tory self-help stuff?'

'Well, most of it. You didn't tell us the interview would be so long.'

'D'you know, that's the second time this week that's happened,' I said with resignation.

We did, in the end, have about two sentences of the answer, which was just about enough. But anyway, everyone was far more interested in what she'd been saying to the children. We used the protester's question about unemployment, but it took a lot of fiddling round with the sound to cut out the bad language.

'Bugger these bloody leftie women,' said the Sound Engineer when he finally managed it. 'Bleeding disgusting language.'

Then he returned to his contemplation of *Men Only*, with all the innocence of a vegetarian vicar at a teetotal wedding.

# 14

## ROMANCE OF VARIOUS KINDS

'Talking of vegetarian weddings,' said my medical friend Bu, 'that's going to be a bit of a problem.'

'What wedding?' said I, slow as ever on the uptake.

'Mine.'

'Yours. You're getting married. Who to?' The obvious question really.

'Richard, you know Richard.'

Of course I knew Richard, he'd been at university with us and had wandered back into our social life some months before.

'That was a bit quick, wasn't it?'

She shrugged. 'Anyway,' she went on, 'catering is going to be a problem. We'll have to have some vegetarian food. But Richard's people won't want that.'

'You seem to have it all worked out.'

'Well, what I do want, is for you to be bridesmaid.'

'You want what? You don't know what it is you're asking,' I squeaked. 'Bridesmaid, I'm too old to be a bridesmaid. You want a little blonde five-year-old toddling behind you.' I was beginning to wake up now. 'What on earth did your parents say?' Bu's Dad is Sikh and her mother Hindu. Richard's family are Welsh Chapel, Welsh-speaking Chapel at that.

'Oddly enough, my aunts, I mean, it's my aunts really who're traditional, my aunts are highly relieved that I'm not on the shelf.'

'But you're not even thirty . . .'

'Ah, well. Anyway, can you be bridesmaid? It's a registry office do, and then we'll have a big party and things. It's in three weeks. Before anyone starts thinking up lots of good objections.'

Although the wedding was going to be at Marylebone Registry Office, Bu had decided to wear a traditional red sari. She'd been living in a hospital flat, and for the night before the Big Day came to stay with me. Richard had a house in Highgate which they'd been busy converting.

The wedding day dawned, as all these days are supposed to, lovely and bright. I toddled in with the traditional nice boiled egg. 'Wake up, honeybunch.'

She sat up. 'I've just remembered, we haven't got any soft drinks.'

'Does it matter?' I asked. 'You just need some Coke for the kids.'

'My aunts are all teetotal.' Hasty phone calls to minicab firm to please go and buy large quantities of fruit juice. Phone rings, it's Richard.

'No, you can't talk to her, it's unlucky.'

Richard gave up with unusual resignation.

Bu's sari was rather creased, so we decided to iron it. Have you ever tried to iron a sari? About three miles of silk drapes itself

193

round the living-room while you struggle with the foot of it on the ironing board. With the sari goes a choli, a light short blouse.

'This isn't really the right one for this sari,' said Bu. Then, 'Oh dear.' It was clearly too small. We looked at it in alarm, there was only an hour to go, no time to get a replacement.

'Can you sew?' Bu asked. I shook my head. We looked at the top again. 'I think,' she said, 'we could let those side seams out. Have you any scissors?' In the end we had to use a scalpel to cut the thread.

Once the top was on and the sari draped round it, the hasty alterations didn't show. Bu tinkled with jewellery given by her family. She stood in front of the mirror, head to toe in red and gold, carefully painting a bright red line down the parting of her hair. 'Very traditional,' she said with satisfaction.

'What *is* that red stuff?' I asked curiously, with visions of heaven knows what exotica from the Romantic East.

'Your lipstick,' she said. 'Mine's too dark.' Then she fixed a circular gold plaque to hang in the middle of her forehead. It was quite a contrast with her usual suited, white-coated, stethoscope and air-call bleep image.

'You look', I said truthfully, 'quite ravishing.'

We arrived at the registry office to find it already mobbed with relatives. Bu's aunts were all in saris, looking magnificently colourful, Richard's female relatives equally festive in large brilliant hats. Of Richard himself there was no sign. We all trooped inside and sat in the waiting room. The aunts kept together along one wall like a flock of birds. Richard's mother was having an animated four-way conversation with Bu's mum in a mixture, as far as I could tell, of English, Hindi, Welsh and a great deal of gesticulating.

'I must say', said Bu, who was perched on the extreme edge of a chair, trying not to disturb the elaborate folds of her sari, 'that Richard won't now be able to talk about women always being late.'

'Late for his own wedding indeed,' said Richard's uncle Joseph in a strong Welsh accent. At that point the groom arrived, to a mixture of trilingual abuse.

The civil ceremony was like all such ceremonies. There were a few tears.

'I don't know what the custom is,' said the Registrar, looking round, 'but in England it's usual to kiss the bride.' Richard kissed Bu rather tentatively on the cheek. Then photos inside, of them pretending to sign the register — you're not allowed to film the real signing. Then more photos outside, and people piling into cars, and much fluttering of hankies and confetti.

The reception indicated why Bu had not wanted a child bridesmaid. I had to *work* for my dinner. The do was in two parts, first in their new home, and then a dinner and dance at Kenwood House.

Richard's mother was presiding over the catering at their home. This seemed pretty lavish, as we were going on to dinner: scores of bottles of champagne, not to mention fruit juice, plates piled high with samosas (a bit like spicy Cornish pasties), slabs of a bright green sweetie, which I avoided, but the aunts seemed to enjoy, as well as vol-au-vents and all the conventional snacks.

'Good,' she said, as I approached, hoping for a drink. 'Just the person I need.' I left the kitchen laden with trays of things to pass round. Out of the corner of my eye I saw the best man being equally employed. Bu's female relatives had settled down in the living-room, still all sitting together, so we shuttled back and forth plying them with goodies.

Bu's sister, a civil servant, pulled me into a corner.

'Richard's uncle keeps giving me grapefruit juice,' she said plaintively, hitching up her sari with the unease of one considerably more used to jeans. 'Any chance of a drink?'

I fetched her some champagne. Then I noticed a couple of the allegedly teetotal aunts gently pouring champagne from an unclaimed glass into their fruit juice. As I wasn't quite sure what protocol ordained, I brought another couple of glasses full of fizz and left them strategically placed for discreet refills.

'Shall we go and talk to Rabbit?' suggested Bu.

Rabbit lives in a hutch at the bottom of the garden. Rabbits quite often do. He was a research rabbit who used to live in a laboratory at the hospital where he was fed growth hormones. When the project was finished he would normally have been put down, but Bu adopted him and brought him home. Rabbit, never having met another rabbit, thinks he's human and gets very sulky if left out of things. He looked at us hopefully.

195

'Shall we give him some champagne?' suggested Richard.

'Do rabbits like champagne?' I asked sceptically.

'Well, he likes beer.'

We filled the feeding dish with best vintage Moet & Chandon and watched Rabbit curiously. He liked it.

'Shall we let him out for a bit?' proposed Bu. It seemed like a good idea at the time, so out Rabbit came. He stood still for a moment then wobbled off round the lawn. He was having noticeable difficulty co-ordinating his legs.

'Do you think we gave him too much?' asked Bu redundantly. 'Perhaps I'd better put him back in his hutch.'

She moved over to try and pick him up. But Rabbit didn't want to be swept out of the way and miss all the activity. Suddenly he started tearing round the lawn, diving past the wedding guests who had come out of the house to watch the fun. Bu raced after him, sari flying and jewellery tinkling; Richard cut in to try and catch him with a rugby tackle, missed and landed in a rose bush. Rabbit then shot under a garden table and sat there looking complacent, if somewhat cross-eyed.

'Why don't you just leave him out?' I asked.

'Well, he might get away,' said Bu. 'And after all that growth hormone I don't know if it would be a very good idea if he got together with a lady rabbit. There'd probably be a plague of giant bunnies terrorising North London.'

'Perhaps we should give him some more champagne?' suggested Richard.

'But he's practically paralytic already,' I protested.

However, we shoved another saucerful under the table. Rabbit drank it with every sign of enjoyment. Then the assembled wedding guests watched anxiously as Rabbit tottered a few further steps before sinking into a small furry heap. Richard scooped up the recumbent bunny and put him back in his hutch, where he lay snoring loudly. Bu filled his bowl with water.

'He'll have a dreadful hangover tomorrow,' she said.

'Well, he'll be in good company,' giggled Richard.

Meanwhile, the aunts, who had all brought evening dresses with them, went upstairs to change in the master bedroom. This was Bu and Richard's pride and joy. They had decorated it themselves and installed an exotic bed, built into the floor, complete with stereo. Not content with that, they'd gone on to construct a platform at one end of the room, fitted with an enormous sunken bath. The whole room was lined with with gold-framed mirrors and Indian miniature prints. The aunts returned with slightly stunned expressions.

'*Je kamra tho ek nachklane jasa lagta hae,*' said the most imposing auntie to Bu's mum. Or words to that general effect.

'What's that?' asked Richard's Auntie Di.

'She means it's a very pretty bedroom,' said the best man, who spoke Hindi.

Auntie Di smiled. 'Yes, isn't it lovely? Just like out of one of those American films. Tell her I think so too.'

Bu was looking more than a shade uneasy.

'What did she really say?' I murmured to the best man, drawing him aside.

'That it looked like a *nautchgana* — something between a geisha house and a brothel.'

I spluttered into my glass, watching the two aunts smiling and nodding at each other in a flurry of linguistic chaos.

Bu joined us. 'I never knew my aunt even knew what a *nautchgana* was,' she said in slightly shocked tones.

'Another myth shattered,' the best man replied unsympathetically.

The next stage of the operation was a much more formal affair at Kenwood House, including scores of people who hadn't been to the registry office. Bu, Richard and I went on first. I took Bu off to the ladies to fix her hair. With her own bathroom stacked wall to wall with aunts, it was really much more peaceful here.

Kenwood House, set in a park, and just a mile from their home, was the perfect spot for a wedding reception. It was a brilliant evening if a bit chilly, and people stood around in self-consciously elegant attitudes, sipping wine and gazing over the lawn to the lake and woods below.

The dinner was a mixture of foods to cope with a variety of tastes ranging from a very Welsh 'Nothing fancy, dear' to Indian vegetarian. Speeches were in English, Hindi and Welsh, and there was a continual buzz as people translated for their neighbours. At least the language barrier meant that only half the guests realised the blushing bridegroom had forgotten to toast the bride's parents.

The happy couple were going to Barbados for their honeymoon, and were supposed to be spending the night at an airport hotel.

'But we're just going to go back home for tonight,' Bu confided to me in a whisper.

'Why? I thought you were all packed.'

'Well, we are, but I'm very worried about Rabbit, so think we'd better just make sure he's all right.'

So they shot off in their car, amid showers of rice and confetti, back home to nurse the comatose bunny.

Next day Bu phoned me at dawn. 'We're just on our way to the airport. Good party, wasn't it?'

'How's Rabbit?'

'Oh, he's fine,' she reassured me.

'That's nice,' I said, and groped my way to the bathroom to try to find an aspirin. Lucky Rabbit.

Romance seemed to be kind of generally flying around the air. I hadn't seen Julie for some time, and this usually indicated she was in the throes of yet another grand passion. Indeed, even my own quiet little love life had been blooming somewhat of late, with Current Bloke much addicted to sending flowers. I was just arranging the latest floral tribute when Julie rang up.

'I've got your dress,' she said.

'What dress?'

'*The* dress — the one that had toothpaste on it.'

'It's so long since I've seen that dress', I said with some venom, 'that I'd forgotten I ever possessed it.'

But finally I surrendered with as much grace as I could drag out, and Julie came over for dinner.

'They got all the toothpaste out,' she said cheerfully. 'Cost me nine quid.' She looked at me hopefully.

'Thanks,' was the only reply I could muster. I thought nine quid was quite reasonable for a year's hire of my nice black dress.

Julie accepted a drink and settled on the settee with an expectant air. 'Did you meet anyone nice at the Tory conference?'

'I was working so hard at that conference, I didn't have time to notice who I met.'

'Oh. That's sad.' She still had a keen aura of excitement.
'Well, are you going to tell me?' I finally asked.
'Tell you what?'
'You're sitting there like a hen about to lay an egg. What's happened? Is it that man you were on about?'
She fiddled with her glass. 'He's very nice.'
'And?' I began to see why in the Middle Ages they used torture to get their information. I seemed constantly to be quizzing Julie with exaggerated politeness while my fingers itched to start on the thumbscrews.
'He's lovely.' She stroked her hair and gazed into nothingness with a faintly ecstatic sort of look. Then she continued, 'Well, I'm not really supposed to tell anyone, but he's offered me a smashing job.'
'I thought you were going to say he'd proposed. It seems to be the season for it.'
'Well, I think he might. But, you know I said he was rich?'
'Mmmmmm,' I replied enviously.
'He wants me to work as a kind of personal assistant and go to Japan with him. He's collecting material for a history of the Samurai.'
'But do you want to give up market research? I thought you liked it?'
'Well, yes, but with this job I'll get all over the world. I'll really be a kind of writer.'
I went to have a look at what was in the oven, to give myself time to think. Then said, 'Look, I haven't met the man, but I'd have thought it all sounds a bit odd. What about extra-curricular activity?'
She looked blank. 'I don't think he's like that.'
'*Everyone's* like that. Unless they've got quite different tastes.'
'Why do you always think the worst of people? He's never touched me.'
'Tell me more,' I pleaded.
'Well, I met him ages ago. And he's very well off.'
'Has he got a job?'
'He's a lawyer. He's American, incidentally. Anyway, he asked me out, and we get on very well, and then he suggested I come to Japan with him.'

'But if he's all that keen on you why doesn't he just offer to pay for your trip?'

'I suspect,' said Julie confidingly, 'it's got something to do with a PA being tax deductible or something.'

'I am beginning to see,' I said slowly, 'how you got kidnapped that last time.'

'That's not the same thing at all. Anyway, Japan's civilised.'

'When are you going?'

'As soon as I sort out my flat and so on.'

There didn't seem to be much else to say, so I let the subject drop. But I was extremely worried. I wondered whether to phone Julie's family, but after all, the woman was well past her teens and surely able to look after herself.

Then she phoned up again. 'When are you off?' I asked with an uncharacteristically heavy lack of enthusiasm.

'Day after tomorrow. I'm ringing to say goodbye for now.'

'Look, Julie . . .'

'It's okay. I know what you're going to say. But I took your advice. My dad came down to London to meet him, and he's checked out his background.' There was a pause. 'He's married,' said Julie flatly.

'But you're still going?'

'Yes, boring isn't it? He really does want a PA; that's what all the chat-up was for. It seems good researchers are scarcer than sexy mistresses. And with all that, it really is the most marvellous job.'

'Still, be careful,' I said. 'He might expect more than just help with research.'

'His wife's coming too,' she said mournfully. I choked slightly. 'Still,' she said, brightening up, 'he's got rather a nice brother. And I'm getting paid a fortune.'

Two months later I got a postcard from Tokyo. 'Having a sensational time. Work great fun; going to India next week. Julie. PS I've met this smashing bloke.'

Julie's postcards continued to arrive at the office with mildly depressing frequency. When the post-room assistant handed over a batch ranging from Delhi to the Seychelles, I dumped them all in the wastebin and went to hunt for the coffee trolley. I finally found it on the ground floor; it always comes to the Newsroom last, after it's been round all the technical departments. By that time there's hardly a sandwich left. I scooped up a lonely bacon roll just ahead of the hungry News Editor.

'Sixteen pence, love,' said the tealady.

'What?' In disbelief.

'It's gone up again.'

I paid up and stayed by the trolley eating slowly, listening to a blonde from accounts describe the passionate encounter she'd had with one of my colleagues the night before. I didn't believe a word of it.

The News Editor listened with equal scepticism.

Finally, he said, 'I've got a nice little job for you. Finish that sandwich and get going.'

I raised an interrogative eyebrow.

'The Cartoonists' Club gives an annual award to the public figure who's provided them with the most inspiration in the past year. This time it's going to a bear.'

'Who?'

'A bear, you know, one of the things with four legs and paws. Now hop along to it like a good girl. By the way, you'll be using ENG.'

ENG stands for electronic news gathering equipment. It had just been introduced for general use on the news and was everyone's latest toy. From a news point of view it can be a magic Santa Claus. The picture is recorded electronically, on tape, so it doesn't have to go through labs for development, like film. This means a story can be shot far later on in the day, much nearer the time the news goes on the air. At present both film and ENG are used, with film still in the majority, but ENG is the equipment of the future. In this particular instance, it meant we could 'film' safely till about twenty past twelve and still get the story on *News at One*.

The bear in question was called Hercules; he had shot to fame some months previously when he had done a bunk in the Hebrides. He had finally been recaptured, some twenty stone lighter than his usual fifty stone weight, the Hebrides being a bit short on protein sustenance. Since then, he'd been much in demand on TV chat shows and the like.

This morning the Metropolitan Police were showing an understandable reluctance to have a bear wandering around their patch. Several large and curiously bear-like coppers were standing around in attitudes of expectation. I asked one of them what was going on.

'It's the Wild Animals Act; the owners could get fined four hundred pounds.'

From the number of press and telly types languishing on the icy pavement, it seemed to me that the publicity would be cheap at twice the price.

The bear arrived in its own specially converted bus, which was promptly mobbed by sightseers and press. After a lot of chit-chat from the police with Hercules' owner, and then with the rampaging media, reporters and photographers were herded back inside the pub, and corralled behind benches while Hercules was led in to get his prize.

As a treat he was given a pint of Babycham, but to the collective disgust of the photographers he turned his back on all of us to drink it in decent privacy.

There were at least fifty journalists packed into the tiny bar. 'Watch our lights,' I kept saying, but nobody took any notice. The inevitable happened: someone kicked the plug and the lights went out. The pub was now lit by only dim side lamps. Hercules had had enough; he turned and made for the door. Finally he was persuaded back inside for two minutes flat, when he was hastily presented with his award, for the benefit of photographers.

'Well, that's that,' said my Cameraman, with relief.

'Shall we try and do a sort of interview, in his cage?' I asked, rather hoping to be told this wasn't on.

'Now, that's not at all a bad idea,' said the Cameraman to my horror. Hercules' owner was equally cheerful about it, so we all climbed into the bus, the Cameraman propelling me relentlessly in front of him. Possibly as a shield.

'Nice bear,' I said tentatively. Hercules lumbered over.

'He wants to wrestle,' said his owner. 'Get out the cage.' We left precipitately. 'I'll just give him some Coca-Cola,' said the owner, proceeding to fill a good-sized enamel bucket.

'Is that animal safe?' I asked.

'Oh, he's fine.'

I didn't believe this, but anyway we all got back into the cage again. Hercules sat on the floor relishing his Coke.

'Can I stroke him?' I asked, trying to prove to myself that I wasn't scared stiff.

'Yes, sure, he's had his lunch.'

The bear's hair was quite unexpectedly soft and thick, silky too, and smelt rather like an old fur coat, musty but not unpleasant.

'We use shampoo,' explained his owner.

Then Hercules finished his Coke and looked round for someone to play with. He stretched out a large paw. 'I think it's time to go,' I said as we backed out with indecorous haste.

'Isn't he lovely?' said the Cameraman as we walked back to the car.

'He's not really my type,' I replied. 'but I wouldn't mind a fur coat like that in this weather.'

I'd never really realised how cold winter could be till I became a reporter. In most jobs you scamper from home, to bus or tube, then toddle into a nice warm office. But with hour after hour hanging about outside someone's flat, or on the pavement at Number Ten, or struggling across wet and muddy fields, you become very conscious of the changing seasons.

Christmas and New Year working tends to be very much a case of drawing the short straw; the News Desk assistant sidles over and says in a hopeful sort of fashion, 'Can you work Christmas this year?' It's not so bad if a good story breaks and you're chasing off somewhere, but if it's quiet and you finish early, it can be extremely depressing. New Year isn't so bad, but on both those dates the news seems to conspire against you. If it's going to happen, it'll happen at the wrong moment.

It was a nice, crisp New Year's Eve. I was on late duty, a shift that runs from two o'clock until ten thirty at night. Absolutely nothing was happening, and I'd spent my entire shift sitting in the Newsroom reading back numbers of everything from the *Economist* to *Playgirl*. New Year's Eve and not a drink all day. At ten thirty, the end of the shift, I sighed with relief.

'Let's get a drink,' said a similarly bored and sober colleague. We went wearily to the bar. 'Are you on tomorrow?' I shook my head.

'Well, then, let's have some champagne.' We bought a bottle of champagne and settled in a corner in a state of rapidly increasing relaxation.

'How I hate New Years,' I said.

At about eleven I was just making my first tentative move towards going home when the phone went. 'For you.'

A wave of guilt hit me. I'd forgotten I'd arranged to meet Current Bloke, and he was probably sitting outside my flat.

'Hello.'

'Oh good, I thought you'd gone.' It was the News Desk. 'A bomb's gone off in the West End. Can you come down here?'

'Bloody hell,' I said with some feeling. 'It had to happen, didn't it.'

I grabbed my coat and sped for the lift, leaving my colleague cheerfully finishing off the bottle, his tie comfortably loosened.

Down in the Newsroom problems began to mount. The film crews had all technically gone off duty, but luckily one crew had stayed on in the bar and they were getting ready to go to the site of the blast. But we didn't have any lights, and it was far too dark to film without them.

'I'll get lights on their way to you,' said the News Editor. 'You should have them in an hour.'

We climbed morosely into the camera car.

'Where's he going to get lights from at this hour?' asked the Sound Recordist.

'We'll just have to use the BBC's.'

'If they've got any.'

If the opposition has lights you can jump in on their filming, but of course you're restricted to filming what they film. And it's no good for eye-witnesses and so on.

We arrived in the West End, and parked the car. The police already had white tapes up to keep back the public. I showed my press pass and they directed us round another way. Finally we arrived at the narrow street where the bomb had gone off. The high houses, with small windows, seemed to lean inwards.

It had been in a car, and the two passengers were both dead.

'Looks like an own-goal,' said the Cameraman.

An own-goal is when someone carrying a bomb to plant accidentally blows himself up instead. The car was crumpled on one side of the road and broken glass was everywhere. The press were being kept well back while forensic experts went over the wreckage. A little crowd of people from flats opposite stood on the pavement watching. The BBC were filming away, with lights, so we filmed away too. Meanwhile I went off to find anyone who'd seen what happened.

Quite a few neighbours had good stories to tell, and I persuaded a couple of them to stay up for a bit till our lights arrived. The opposition had already spoken to eyewitnesses, so we couldn't, as it were, jump on their bandwagon for lights.

The hours ticked on. A police spokesman gave a noncommittal statement. The BBC finished and pushed off.

It was nearly two o'clock; my eye-witnesses said they were fed up waiting, and were going home. I took their addresses so they could be followed up next day.

'Well, I think we might as well go too,' said the Cameraman.

'But what about the lights? He'll be on his way, he must be nearly here. I don't really like just to go off.'

So, out of a bemused sense of duty, we hung around for another fifteen minutes, till the Lights Man arrived. Told him it was all over, and said goodnight.

I went back to the office and left a note for the News Desk telling them what time the lights had arrived, and giving the eye-witnesses' addresses. Then back to the flat.

It was only when I approached my front door that I was suddenly horror-stricken. I'd totally forgotten Current Bloke. On my doorstep was a bottle of champagne (another one) with a note pinned to it: 'Waited an hour, where were you? Your office said you'd gone home.'

It was now close to three in the morning, but the note had a slightly emphatic tone about it. I was just about to pick up the phone and start apologising when it rang.

'Where were you?'

'I've been on a story — that bomb in Mayfair.'

'Your office said you'd gone home.'

'Well, who did you speak to?' Always attack when you feel in the wrong.

'I don't know.'

'Well, they probably had no idea what I was doing. People are always saying other people have gone home.'

'Oh. Can I come over?'

'It's three o'clock.'

205

'So?'

'Well, I suppose so,' trying to sound suitably enthusiastic, 'but just for a bit. I might have to work tomorrow on that story.'

I shoved the champagne in the fridge and settled down with some strong black coffee. Half an hour went by. Nobody turned up. I phoned his flat. No answer. I was beginning to think this was a not so subtle way of getting his own back when the phone went again.

'Pip pip pip.' Coin box.

'Hello, hello. You're not going to believe this. I slipped on the ice getting to my car. I'm at the Middlesex casualty. They think my arm's broken, I'm waiting for an X-ray.'

'Oh no.' I could feel what I was being expected to offer, but couldn't manage to sound enthusiastic.

'Would you,' I said in a martyred tone, 'like me to come down and sit with you?'

'Well, that's very kind.'

'I might have difficulty getting a cab . . .'

'Well, of course, if you don't want to . . .'

Twenty minutes later I was huddled in a cab, heading back into central London.

'Quite a time you seem to be having,' laughed the chatty driver.

The casualty department was cold, echoing and deserted, except for one nurse on Admissions.

'Have you got Mr So and So with a broken arm?'

She looked down a list. 'We've been a bit busy. Ah, there. He'll be a few minutes.'

'Seems quiet enough now.'

'You should have seen it an hour ago.'

I settled down to wait, finally falling asleep.

'Hi.'

'How's the arm?'

'Oh, just a sprain.' This with the sort of soppy grin that's supposed to be bewitching.

'I thought you said it was broken.'

He looked at me as if he felt he were not getting the attention he deserved. 'Well, it hurt as if it were broken.'

'So what would you like to do?' I asked with a misguided rush of sympathy.

'I'll run you home, then let's have a drink to celebrate the New Year.'

So once again that night I headed for Highgate. Dawn was breaking in a miserable sort of fashion as we went up the hill. Current Bloke steered cautiously with one hand.

Once inside Bloke sprawled on the sofa, in the attitude of one clearly expecting to be waited on hand and foot, while I went to get the champagne. I was feeling distinctly unfestive. I opened it at the kitchen sink — I'd no wish to get fizz all over my nice new furniture.

'Would you like some scrambled egg?' I called. No answer. I went back to the living-room to find a totally unconscious form occupying the entire sofa.

'Wake up!' I shook him. Dead to the world. So I thumped him sadistically in the ribs. He turned over: quite unconscious, a seraphic smile on his face.

'Happy New Year,' I muttered, swallowing my champagne, and went to bed.

Four hours later I was on the phone to the News Desk.

'. . . so the lights didn't get there till it was more or less all over.'

'Well, anyway, thanks very much,' said the News Editor.

'Shall I come in and follow the story on?'

'No. You were up too late, I'll give it to someone else.'

'But I want to!'

'No, take your day off. Have a rest. You can't have been home till three.'

As this was a slight understatement, I left the conversation there, and toddled disconsolately into the living-room to see how the Sleeping Beauty was doing. Still sleeping.

I went back to bed and turned on the early news. Last night's blast wasn't even the top story; less than twelve hours later it was already yesterday's news. I switched off the radio, and went gratefully to sleep.